ON THE DESTINY OF NATIONS

ALSO BY DENNIS PEACOCKE

Winning the Battle for the Minds of Men, 1987

Doing Business God's Way, 1995

The Emperor Has No Clothes, 2003

ON THE
DESTINY
OF
NATIONS

RESOLVING OUR ECONOMIC CRISIS

DENNIS PEACOCKE

**AN INFORMED CHRISTIAN CHALLENGE
TO ABSURD ECONOMIC POLICIES,
LEFT-RIGHT POLITICAL GAMES, AND
A FREQUENTLY IRRELEVANT CHURCH**

REBUILD
Santa Rosa, California

Published in the United States by REBUILD
Santa Rosa, CA
Library of Congress Cataloguing-in-Publication Data

Peacocke, Dennis.
    On the Destiny of Nations: Resolving Our Economic Crisis/ Dennis Peacocke.
        p. cm.
    1. Economics. 2. Christianity. 3. Public Policy. I. Title.

Library of Congress Control Number: 2012910065

ISBN 978-1-8870-2106-7

Unless otherwise noted, Scripture quotations are from the New American Standard Bible (NASB)®. Scripture quotations taken from the New American Standard Bible®, Copyright © 1960, 1962, 1963, 1968, 1971, 1972, 1973, 1975, 1977, 1995 by The Lockman Foundation. Used by permission. (www.Lockman.org)

Printed in the United States of America

Designed by: Kathyjo Varco

Editing by: Mary C. Lewis, MCL Editing, Etc.

Photograph on page 183, copyright © 2012 by Tom Jackson

10 9 8 7 6 5 4 3 2 1

First Edition

DEDICATION

"All the ends of the earth will remember and turn to the Lord And all the families of the nations will worship before You. For the kingdom is the Lord's and He rules over the nations."
Psalm 22:27-29

To the emerging leaders and thinkers of the nations and the lovers of God's earth and its people who, like myself, see the continuing slide downward into cultural madness; and to large segments of the church, either oblivious to this reality or trapped in a paralysis as to what to do about it. This is a defining moment for you, and as the following quote tells us, a defining moment for our modern "experiment" in the West of societies governed without an agreed upon set of common values and agreed upon spiritual assumptions......and to the Lord for faithfully guiding Jan and I together in one heart through this process.

> "We begin by noting that this is a unique cultural moment. Beneath all of the other major cultures were religious assumptions, whether these came from Hinduism, Islam, or Christianity itself. There are no such religious assumptions beneath our culture, however, and this is the first time any major civilization has attempted to build itself in this way."
>
> David Wells, *No Place for Truth*, 1994, p. 80

TABLE OF CONTENTS

ACKNOWLEDGMENTS

With deep gratitude to my editors and manuscript aides, James Jankowiak, Lynn Shubunka, Roxanne Trujillo and Mary Lewis, for their wonderfully applied insights; to the scriptural additions by Bruce Billington and Thomas Jackson; to my faithful brothers who challenged me to finish the project carefully before the release of this book; to Jeff and Lakita Wright, whose insight and support were invaluable; and to the Holy Spirit who graciously energized and supported me in this most challenging set of circumstances surrounding the whole project. Words cannot say....

INTRODUCTION

"...He will sit on His glorious throne. All the nations will be gathered before Him; and He will separate them from one another, as the shepherd separates the sheep from the goats;"

Matthew 25:31-32

Nations, like people, have destinies. Today, the nations of the world are confronted with a global crisis, some more than others. Yet, technology and global markets have tied us all together. This economic crisis is, at its heart, a values crisis. It is sustainable values that emanate from love that will elevate one person, one community, or one nation above the others as the emerging leaders of the new order guide us forward. Make no mistake: this economic crisis signals a pivotal moment of change for the people and nations of the earth. For the nations, it is a learning opportunity and a spiritual portal:

"For when the earth experiences Your judgments
The inhabitants of the world learn righteousness."

Isaiah 26:9

Economics, because it is the organizing system of man's labor, time, material possessions, and lifestyle, is about far more than just money, things, or power. It is about our hopes for ourselves and our posterity and how we can find fulfillment in the release of our labor. It is also the financial platform from which we build the other things in life, which transcend the material world. Therefore, when there is a major economic crisis, stability, provision, and hope are at risk for people and nations. This is a book about the challenging necessity of building a values-based economy that offers the possibility of sustained prosperity for the greatest number of people as a result of love-driven values.

The ideas and systems that brought us to this moment are tottering and increasingly insecure. They need careful scrutiny and attention.

Who is going to help us sort them out and help clarify their usefulness? The leaders of the next phase of human history and man's institutions have inherited that responsibility. They will have to sort out the ideas, values, and solutions that will lead the nations out of this crisis. Whole nations will surge forward or slump backward based on the wisdom of these leaders. Is it possible that "the first shall be last and the last shall be first"[1] in this process? Indeed.

This book is written by a Christian to both Christians and everyone else who cares about people, the earth, and the ultimate values that define and create the majesty and limitations of mankind. It is a hard read because the issues we must plow through and sort out require our fullest attention and the courage to define and deploy unpopular stands in the midst of self-interest and confusion. This is a book about defining moments and severe challenges that demand pain and reveal character. Ultimately, it is about partnering with God to bring redemption to people and the social systems of their nations.

Winston Churchill, Prime Minister of England and major historic figure of World War II, in England's darkest moment of the war, offered to his nation a policy of "blood, sweat, and tears." I have a similar challenge to those who choose to plow through the tough issues of this book: What will you do in your spheres of influence and leadership to help guide others across these sharp-edged times to a safer place? I am also inviting the readers of this book, Christian or not, to a kind of global "family meeting," wherein I am directly addressing the more than one billion believers in the world to more clearly see and take a far greater responsibility for the political-economic structures of their nations. May it be leadership that offers us all the chance to attain sustainable prosperity and the ability to please and glorify our Creator.

---

1. See Matthew 20:16.

CHAPTER 1

THE CURRENT CRISIS AND THE SEARCH
FOR A VALUES-BASED ECONOMIC ORDER

"'Teacher, which is the greatest commandment in the Law?'
And He said to them, "You Shall Love The Lord Your God With
All Your Heart, And With All Your Soul, And With All Your Mind."
This is the great and foremost commandment. The second is
like it, "You Shall Love Your Neighbor As Yourself." On these two
commandments depend the whole law and the Prophets.'"

Matthew 22:36-40

The core premise of this book is simple. In Christ's defining and summing up into a single concept the meaning and demands of the entire Scriptures, He offers to mankind the most superior value-base for all of man's conduct and social constructs ever given. To attempt to build our political or economic order on any other supreme guideline is an exercise in futility at best and cruelty at worst. This quest to honor God's values, which are rooted in love, and to honor our neighbor with the highest good we could conceive for ourselves stands as the foundation of what I choose to call "Kingdom Economics." It is the economic construct of what the King Himself says is the foundation stone of His emerging eternal Kingdom—honor God and honor one another. Ultimately, to profoundly honor someone places us squarely on the pathway to *agape* love.

Mankind should measure his political-economic order by this standard, be it capitalism, socialism, or any other economic system set forth for our allegiance. Systems are built upon values, defined or undefined, and my intention is to argue for the constructing of an economic system offering the greatest possibility for aligning itself with Christ's standard of love. To call it by the name of any of the current systems is to miss the point. It must transcend them all, while recognizing the best within them, because God's Kingdom and His economic values transcend them all.

My second major premise is that secular society is committing suicide in its attempt to keep spiritual values out of the public square in terms of affecting its culture and social systems. As secularism gains momentum the cultures of the Western world are manifesting the results: economic crisis due to the corruption of the financial sector's values and the civil government's seemingly unending need for increased control over the lives of their citizens; seriously declining birth rates while at the same time the tidal wave of retirements from the baby boomers is about to place huge demands on entitlement programs and defunded retirement programs; massive disintegration of the traditional family units with half the marriages ending in divorce, increasing numbers of children being born out of wedlock, and a third of the adult population living together out of wedlock for sheer fear of making long-term commitments.

Where does secularism expect the stabilizing values of society to come from? Surely not the political parties, whose primary value is the pragmatism of winning elections. Perhaps they are looking for them to come from their "sanitized" public school systems where spiritual values are illegal to discuss, and their supreme moral value is the toleration of all people's values as long as they are held with "conviction and sincerity". Maybe it is from the universities who view religion and its values as superstitions of weak people incapable of living in the reality of reason and logic. Maybe it's from the media, or the youth culture, which has virtually no experience of what values cause a full life to be lived with enduring dignity.

Secularism's demand that all spiritual values from their Judeo-Christian heritage are to be kept outside of the major influence of their cultures and the management of their social systems is guaranteeing their own demise. However, beyond all these criticisms, much of the church has tacitly permitted this to happen as they quietly agreed that religion was a "private" issue and one to be only carefully injected into public discussions outside of their own church or religious circles. This then takes us to our third major premise.

In my opinion, our attempts to "disciple the nations" according to Christ's Great Commission of Matthew 28:18-20, has left much to be desired. While gratefully conceding the heroic efforts of multitudes of saints, God has seemingly had to frequently go around what we have done in the nations in order to more fully reveal Himself to the people of the earth. So I am saying to those of you who may stand outside, for now, of our faith to listen patiently as I sometimes encourage, sometimes scold, and sometimes plead with others of our faith to think through the tenets of our faith more deeply. I am calling all of us to engage where possible what Christ has given to us as citizens of His Kingdom and citizens of our nations as we attempt to contribute to the betterment of both.

My fourth major premise, which we will come back to shortly, is that this economic crisis is not a mere "recession". It is the beginning of a global economic reset which God will powerfully use to reorder systems, reinsert within the Christian community a love for people and the desire to serve and influence them with the values and principles of God's Kingdom, and reveal a whole new set of global leaders who respond to a more fully integrated social order.

If we Christians respond redemptively it will change us, our churches, and our nations. If we do not respond, or respond foolishly, it will hinder and further isolate our witness to the world. Our challenge is to help reveal Christ's relevance to the whole of the human condition as a King who inaugurated a Kingdom with comprehensive answers to the sins and infrastructures of the world. Nevertheless, we will not respond in sufficient numbers or with sufficient answers if we avoid asking ourselves the kind of questions which "trap" us. Indeed, we must be committed enough and imbued with a sufficient sense of personal obligation to do the hard work of study, personal sacrifice, and common unity with others required to honor God in this battle for the minds of men and the quest for sustainable prosperity. So let us begin our journey by asking the questions that have the power to trap us in the yoke of Christ's burden for the nations for which He died.

The ultimate question for Bible-believing Christians, then, is not when God is going to establish His Kingdom on earth; Christ already has.[1] Neither is it the question of when He will return. Alive or dead we will all be caught up in that event. Our most daunting question is: What does He expect of each of us in the various seasons and changing circumstances of our lives, in terms of personal growth, constructive social interaction, and in our roles as citizens of our communities and our nations? Indeed, what must we do before we die to fulfill our destinies assigned by God? Life often seems hard enough without dealing with questions of this magnitude! Yet, the questions remain and the accountability faces us all squarely.

For many of us the issues of our salvation per se are secured already in Christ and His promises. Our challenge is more to the point of where, how, and toward whom are the specific realities of our resident salvation and gifts to be directed? Another challenging question appears for us as wise stewards of our time and as leaders (every believer is modeling—leading—something to someone for good or ill) as well: How do we leverage both our time and our efforts for maximum results? Those questions are most effectively dealt with by asking God to reveal to our hearts the people group or human challenge that has trapped or "imprisoned" us.[2] From whom, or from what cause, must we not walk away without losing our integrity? For me, it is the establishment of His Kingdom on earth through His people in such a compelling way that the rebellious may contend vigorously against us, but they cannot deny the love and cry for justice that drives us, however much they reject the moral demands and lifestyle of self-denial for which His Kingdom calls. What now follows is my knowingly inadequate attempt to lay out that passion for His Kingdom before you and in the process stir up whatever and whoever has "trapped" and captured you.

---

1. Matthew 4:17; Luke 11:20; Luke 21:31-32.
2. Ephesians 3:1.

My divine entrapment began at the point of my intellectual and spiritual awakenings in the 1960s as a student of political theory and economic justice at Berkeley. Those kind of social and economic questions are the stuff of which this current political-economic crisis now entwining the world is made of. This present political morass must be unraveled and released amidst and in spite of the astounding array of confusion afoot in the current context of the left-right paradigms surrounding us. Here is what this will require of us: we believers must learn to think and act biblically rather than being swept away by the convenient and simplistic thinking of the world's "left-right" political worldviews.

Whatever that unraveling requires, one thing is certain: virtually no one in "the real world" expects Christians to be a significant contributing factor to the process. My protest is that their expectations must not stand; we must engage effectively and with utmost leverage. If indeed we have the mind of Christ and the power of the Holy Spirit, to count ourselves out of the untangling and unpleasantries of the crisis, or expect to be rescued from it by Christ, is a negation of our very placement here on earth as priests to the people and salt and light to their needs.

THE BATTLEFIELD OF THE CURRENT CONFLICT

"If I profess with the loudest voice and the clearest exposition every portion of the truth of God except precisely that little point which the world and the devil are at the moment attacking, I am not confessing Christ, however boldly I may be professing Christ. Where the battle rages, there the loyalty of the soldier is proven and to be steady on all the battlefield besides, is merely flight and disgrace if he flinches at that point."

Martin Luther

This book, like many, has gone through multiple revisions. I have been laboring over the last four years to focus specifically on what we can appropriately isolate as the most relevant aspects of the spiritual demise of the Western world in general, and the United States in particular. This is no small task for two prominent reasons: firstly, the secular world rejects any of the claims of Christ upon it, and secondly, the complexities of public policy and the tenets of political freedom biblically require a separation of the institutions of the church and state without walling off the influence of Christianity upon any aspect of culture. In other words, the institution of the church must not attempt to govern civil society yet it must pour into society Christ's values and principles as an act of love and opportunity for redemption. It has been doubly hard for me since the complexities of various aspects of economic policies and theories likewise make a book of this sort, not specifically designed for economists, a real challenge.

Nevertheless, it is my contention that this current economic crisis, though tailor-made by man, is going to be powerfully used of God. This crisis will challenge His church, and the surrounding culture, to severely re-examine their mutual relationship and the consequences of nations' political economies attempting to successfully function devoid of the penetrating spiritual forces of Jesus' admonition to love God and love people. This crisis is exhibit "A" of the consequences of that omission and the blame for it falls on both sides of the relationship— on the church and the secular cultures. By limiting the church's most frequent concerns to the admittedly critical "moral" issues of abortion, pornography, personal sexual morality, and the like, without at the same time heralding Christ's concerns for justice and the empowerment of both the needy and the indolent, we have generally committed a major strategic error contributing to the church's growing social quarantine. The secularists are not stupid. Their brightest ones well know what the Scriptures say about these issues concerning social justice,[3] in spite of their frequent disregard for what the Scriptures say regarding personal morality and character. Any economic system without Christian ethics and values is doomed to de-humanize man as it exploits the most vulnerable.

Here is what I am saying: This economic crisis is God's best current lever to challenge man viscerally since his economic well-being touches every aspect of his life and culture. This crisis has fully engaged the public's attention and will continue to do so for the foreseeable future. My fourth major premise, once again, is that this is no mere

---

3.   Isaiah 58.

"recession"; it is an incredible spiritual opportunity and a time to see the reality of God's provision and intervention in the affairs of man. To miss the engaging of this situation by those Christians able to do so is to fall prey to exactly what the quote from Martin Luther powerfully warned us about at the beginning of this section. May God's people not flinch "precisely at that little point" that we now face.

THE FOUR MAIN POINTS OF OUR FOCUS

The four general areas of this study will therefore focus on the following issues of concern:

1. There are extremely negative economic consequences when the secular forces of the world attempt to function without the "salt and light"[4] of Christ's wisdom addressing their economic presuppositions, ethics, and notions of both environmental and systemic political sustainability. An undiscipled nation is a nation outside of the fuller blessings of Christ and the life giving principles and disciplines making sustainability possible.

2. The "medicating" of the citizens living under the above phenomena grows ever more dangerous. It is numbing their minds with inferior systems of public education, reducing their knowledge of their own history and diminishing the principles required to maintain freedom. It involves media "sound bite" public discussions, void of sufficient content to press the general public into genuine, principle-based thought or discussions, and further erodes our citizens' abilities to produce sufficiently competent public servants to turn things around.

3. There is an ever-expanding centralization of political power in civil government that further encroaches in the lives of its citizens, and brings acute dangers to both their political liberty and economic sustainability.

4. There is a need to address at least five foundational economic principles that must constantly be reinforced within the economic system, all of which deal with freedom, justice, trustworthy stew-

---

4. Matthew 5:13-16.

ardship, and the ongoing possibility of upward economic mobility taking place within the nations of the earth.

MY BACKGROUND AND THINKING PROCESS

As a Christian I am assuming the Scriptures to be God's Word, delivered to man through man, with the inspiration of the Holy Spirit, allowing man to understand their general meaning while recognizing that he has limited claims on his ability to acquire the absolute understanding of them in this dispensation of time.[5] I am further assuming that the Old Testament is the Word of God, holding the same degree of validity as the New Testament but needing interpretation by the Holy Spirit, the New Testament itself, and the experiences of God stewarding His church and His world across history.[6] I am further assuming that the principles of the Old Testament, specifically as they address the nation of Israel and its social structures, serve as the primary point of departure for the extrapolation of economic and political principles which are applicable to the modern world.[7] While I understand that the Law is fulfilled in Christ and in no way is binding upon believers today,[8] God's principles and admonitions to and for man's well-being are universal and therefore ignored at our great peril.

As one who both worked as a research economist and has continued to hold a binding interest in economic theory and application over the last forty-plus years, I do recognize some of the challenges of applying biblical principles, given to a people largely living in an agrarian-based economy and highly de-centralized political system as well, to our modern times. I nevertheless recognize the general application of all truth to mankind since both his inherent nature and the nature of truth itself neither expires nor is made null and void by man's presumptions concerning himself or his technological achievements.

I have been trained intellectually in political theory, opting out of graduate studies as one needing to experience the "real world" apart from academia. I have spent the last forty-five years attempting to

---

5. 1 Corinthians 13:12.
6. Matthew 5:17-20; 2 Timothy 3:16.
7. Matthew 5:17-19.
8. Romans 10:4.

build a truly Christian worldview as I pastored, led church networks, lectured on public policy and economics, and worked on various projects of community development and economic advancement through the schools we have started around the world.

My intellectual orientation is that of a "pre-suppositionalist";[9] that is, one who believes that until we understand one's basic assumptions about the nature of reality and are self-consciously aware of those assumptions, it is difficult if not impossible to either advance a meaningful argument, or have an intelligent discussion which moves toward mutual understanding with others. I will attempt to make my presuppositions clear as we go along in this book and discuss the issues at hand. I am also asserting that political freedom and economic freedom are inseparably linked as has been modeled biblically and acknowledged throughout the liberal traditions of Western thought, most clearly pointed out by Adam Smith and those who followed him. This is a brief history of my background and thought process, which I trust will be helpful as you read the book.

A QUICK LOOK AT THE CURRENT ECONOMIC CRISIS

"The practical consequences of religion can be integrated easily enough into economic analysis, treating religious values as a key influence in shaping a given individual structure of 'preferences.' But the sources of religious belief represent a much less familiar and much less comfortable ground for economic analysis. Yet the successful workings of an economic system may depend heavily on the specific character of religious beliefs that serve to provide normative foundation for the market. Achieving a more efficient economy may depend on having a more 'efficient' religion. A surprising possibility is thus raised: it might not be economists but the theologians who are the most important members of society in determining economic performance."

Robert H. Nelson, *Economics as Religion*, 2001, p. 8

---

9. Proverbs 23:7.

Many have called the current economic crisis a "recession", which generally means a consecutive number of quarterly economic declines in a number of important areas in the overall economy of a nation. Both I and many other people dealing in the realm of economics do not believe that; we believe this is the beginning of a global economic reset which will take place over the next decade or so. It is far more serious than a mere recession. We will be commenting on this assertion as we go through the book. The initial run of the current economic crisis was triggered in the United States by a lethal combination of artificially low interest rates tied to an artificially high housing "bubble", coupled with ridiculously flawed housing loans and driven by shameful greed on the sides of both the federal housing leaders and the financial community. Undergirding this lethal combination was the poor regulation of virtually every facet of oversight, especially in the derivatives market, designed to make sure something like this could not happen. Since all of this is both old news and commonly known, there is little benefit in analyzing this debacle on a deeper level here.

In the longer run, however, there have been major violations of the basic principles of economic and political prudence. These violations make our current "recession" merely a harbinger of the real challenges facing us all in the coming years as the system breaks down on a much more fundamental level. It is called our "debt crisis", but it is much more than just an issue of public financial insolvency.

God has permitted the governments of the world to defund themselves in their attempts to meet needs they are not called to meet and spend the resources of future generations in an act of civil thievery. Many of the nations of the Western world are therefore both culturally and politically increasingly divided as they attempt to explain how they arrived in this condition and the multiple roles of both citizens and civil government in finding the ways out of the problems. The "left-right" culture wars are further entrenching their positions and increasingly locked into many of the same thinking processes that created the problems. Einstein's contention that the level of thinking that creates a problem is insufficient to resolve the problem, has become increasingly imprinted upon much of the current debate.

22

My fifth premise, and my deepest conviction, is that as the central governments of the world are defunded, the real social and economic energy will be found on the local community level. Power is going local and moving away from the centralization process, which has driven the consolidation of social control over the last two centuries. As the centralized governments are defunded, and many of their social systems with them, this will create an historic opportunity for Christians to actually act like the Christians of the first several centuries and step in and care for social needs on a widespread basis. If we do, it will re-center the "salt and light" position God has always wanted His church to take in meeting the needs of people both spiritually and in terms of social service. A true *ecclesia* will emerge that serves society on multiple levels.

Whoever serves most effectively leads the culture. This is what the centralization of civil government was attempting to do in an unbiblical way. It cannot financially afford to do so and it robs the private sector of its biblical mandate for citizens to take a much higher degree of personal responsibility for their neighbors and their community than the ethic of centralization permits or encourages.

ON THE ISSUE OF SUSTAINABLE PROSPERITY

From an overview perspective, it is my desire to see economic prosperity touch the greatest number of people possible based on values that neither corrupt them nor hinder the same opportunities for others or future generations. Biblical prosperity is both spiritual and material, and any definition of prosperity that addresses one without the other is incomplete.[10] Short-term thinking tends to be the cause of many of our social and economic problems and long-term strategic thinking will cure many of the ills created by it, as we will later discuss. Selfish political opportunism feeds on short-term thinking and nothing exposes that kind of thinking more quickly than statesman-like questions coming from truly informed people who are thinking on behalf of the whole of a community and the welfare of the nation.

---

10. Deuteronomy 29:9; Philippians 4:12.

As a generality, in terms of economic emphasis, the left tends to focus on people's security and sense of community and the right tends to focus on the individual's rights to prosper without what it considers undue interference. These two concerns are most quickly joined together in what I have called "Kingdom" economics based on the precepts of Christ's admonition on the greatest commandment already cited. The "one and the many," to use theological language, is always the biblical context upon which all admonitions are built. Created as unique individuals, we are eternally placed in the context of relational community to live out our lives and services to God and one another. Any long-term political-economic solutions must balance the equation of how prosperity must benefit both the individual and the greatest number of people actively participating in the system.

As we further explore the quest for sustainable prosperity for the greatest number of people, we will also discuss the essential need for the possibility of upward economic mobility. That mobility is centered in how economic policy particularly affects the middle classes and their ability to contribute to economic growth through the consumption of what is produced. Economies are likewise based on the levels of trust resident throughout the entire system. When trust breaks down anywhere it tends to spread. Economies are also driven by hope, particularly hope in one's ability to prosper based on increased personal inputs of time, energy, and resource. Hope is to economic investment what love is to relationships.

One of the most important points I want to make in this book, relative to economic theory, is this: Most of the critiques of capitalism are in fact against the abuses of the major corporations in the system in general, and the financial sectors in particular. The major corporations make up only about 20 percent of the GDP (gross domestic product) of most advanced nations' economies. I cannot remember having heard a single vitriolic tirade against those "dirty rotten exploiters from the middle-class business world" that make up at least 80 percent of what capitalism produces. In fact, I do not remember ever having this reality called to my attention, and in my early years at Berkeley, the writings of Marx, Lenin, Eric Fromm, and a host of other anti-capitalist people heavily influenced me. My heart was looking for social justice but concluded it could not be found viewing society from a non-spiritual perspective.

What I earnestly contend is simply this: Wherever political or economic power is concentrated, either in the private or public sector, is where the public most needs proper regulation and guarantees of both liberty, justice, and protection from vested interests. Capitalism, like any and all other economic systems, reflects the value-base of the people participating in the system. In a fallen world there is no perfect system. There are only those systems generally aligned with Christ's admonitions or misaligned with them.

DUAL CITIZENS OF THE NATIONS AND THE KINGDOM OF GOD

We are all citizens of our nations and many of you reading this book identify yourselves as citizens of God's eternal Kingdom. You hold a dual citizenship with dual responsibilities and obligations,[11] sometimes conflicting. I love my nation and I hope all of you have a love for your nation and its people and aspire, as I do, to see it aligned as much as is possible with God's eternal truths and love. However, many Christians have let their sense of responsibility to be salt and light in their nations become a distant obligation, forgetting that Christ commanded us all to "disciple the nations,... teaching them to observe all things whatsoever I have commanded you".[12] While our concern for the things of God's Kingdom properly trumps our concerns for our nation, investing in the social and moral environment of our nations is in fact an investment in spreading the values of the Kingdom and an act of discipling nations as well. To leave our communities and nation alone to follow the convictions of those who have little or no understanding of biblical truth is both irresponsible and a denial of love for humanity.

To see the Kingdom biblically is to understand the "now and not yet" reality of this current dispensation of time.[13] The Kingdom was released by Christ at His first Advent and will be completed and consummated at

---

11. Matthew 22:21; Philippians 3:20; 1 Peter 2:13-17.
12. Matthew 28:18-20.
13. Psalm 145:13; Luke 17:21.

His second coming. In between these dispensations is our time to partner with Him in allowing God's Spirit to use His people to invade time with eternity's values and lifestyle. As citizens of both our nations and God's eternal nation, may we care enough about people and our posterity to invest our time, talent, and treasure in modeling love, informed biblical wisdom, and the courage to stand for both in a fallen world.

THE THREEFOLD CORD: A METHODOLOGY
OF EFFECTIVELY DISCIPLING NATIONS

"And if one can overpower him who is alone, two can resist him. A cord of three strands is not quickly torn apart."

Ecclesiastes 4:12

While our specific focus in this study deals with the analysis of the values and principles required to release sustainable prosperity to the greatest number of people, the underlying thread of engaging people and their social systems with biblical truth (discipling nations) implicitly is woven into the fabric of our journey. The discipling of nations requires the common mobilization of trained believers in the process of releasing the transformation of their own lives and thinking into the personal lives and social systems of the world's cultures. This further presupposes that their efforts will be energized by the specific gifts and callings resident within each believer as they are applying this process. Every believer must release what God has specifically engifted them to contribute to the process of transformation.

As we come to the final chapter in our journey, we will deal with our clearest compass bearings in terms of the most desirable course for an effective methodology that affects and releases the largest number of believers into the kinds of tasks most likely to both disciple nations and remedy our current crisis. In chapter 9 we will therefore re-engage in an overview of the "threefold cord" of discipling nations through 1) compelling prayer, 2) the mobilized transforming of local communities, and 3) the analysis and application of scriptural principles to national social systems.

WHAT I HOPE YOU WILL GET OUT OF THIS BOOK

> "When people say they don't believe in God, it makes sense to ask them which God they don't believe in; when they say they do believe in God, the same question ought to be gently but firmly pressed."
>
> N. T. Wright, *What Saint Paul Really Said*, 1997, p. 161

My earnest desire is that the time invested in both the writing of this book, and your reading of it, will be that we are both better prepared to make a definitive difference to the people and nations of the world. They need answers that transcend mere human wisdom or human self-centeredness. They need Christ and His Kingdom. What I also believe, from the core of my being, is that in the pursuit of demonstrating and encouraging the nations to "come and dine",[14] it will change us as Christians in the process. That is greatly needed as well.

I further hope to share some part of my love and passion for the truths that create and drive political and economic communities. You know, we are going to spend eternity together in community, and I suspect God's eternal truths in these public arenas will not disappear altogether. After all, "He makes all things new,"[15] not all new things. We will go forward into eternity as a community of individual members, bound together within nations comprising His magnificent Kingdom.

---

14. Revelation 3:20.
15. 2 Corinthians 5:17; Revelation 21:5.

CHAPTER 2

ON THE CHALLENGES OF SECULARISM
AND RELIGIOUS DUALISM

The present crisis will define the current generations living through it in a similar way that World War II defined its participating generations. It will continue to have a global impact and as it worsens it could likely provoke major social disruptions. What it most certainly will do is resolve many of the theoretical arguments between liberals and conservatives as to which paths lead to sustainable economic prosperity. That will become obvious because only the truly workable paths will reset and repair the current economic breakdowns. This crisis will be a major "acid test" for what works and what doesn't.

The pragmatically required resolutions will also do something else— expose and severely weaken the secular forces of society who maintain that spiritual arguments have no place in the world of either economics or politically rational policy-making. The secularists have traded in the currencies of prejudice and fear, claiming both the high ground of rationality and the civil protection of society from the forces of religious foolishness and divisiveness. While the forces of religion have historically brought forth numerous destructive issues and actions into their societies, religion certainly has no exclusive corner on that product. For example, all the religious wars and persecutions of history do not compare to what the secular forces of ideology unleashed upon the world in the twentieth century. No, it took the powers of secularism to produce two World Wars, the Korean and Vietnam Wars, and a host of other, smaller wars; the ideological exterminations by the Marxists and fascists of obscene numbers of secular citizens of their own nations; millions of abortions; and the accumulated total extermination of several hundred millions of human beings.

No, secularism, you have convincingly trumped religion's destructiveness. Even the secular forces' own calculations confirm these numbers. This tragic reality, once repeatedly cited, should begin to shift the public discussion and punch holes in their walls of strategically mounted fear and prejudicial language. If this is the safety and rationality that secularism brings to the nations, our wisest response should be "No, thank you."

We believers should neither be offended nor surprised that secularism is firmly established in the context of a New Testament political economy. The New Testament age is the age defined by Christ's invitation to, "whosoever will, may come".[1] This is the age of choice and the freedom to respond out of one's true conscience and not coercion from either secular ideology or religious demands. There are no citizens of God's Kingdom who have not freely chosen to be there, either in the past, the present, or the future. Within the mystery of God's sovereignty and foreknowledge, all beings are given the gift of choice and deceived or coerced only by their own predilections.[2] The game is not rigged: God's *agape* love would not allow it. Christianity, or any other religion which would deny people the freedom of religious conviction, does not accurately represent the heart of our Father. He neither steals nor rapes. Hell will be filled with those who chose that path, however inconceivable that may be to those who chose the other one. I, for one, am equally concerned with zealots from any camp who would steal from us our freedom to dissent lawfully, or freely follow our own conscience, granting that same gift to all others.

Therefore, let it be clear to friends and foes alike, that when we are talking about discipling nations and teaching them to obey the teachings of Christ in a biblical manner, that process cannot be forced in the

1. Matthew 22:9-10; Revelation 3:20; 22:17.
2. Deuteronomy 30:19; Joshua 24:15.

political context. It can only be modeled by our own communities and powerfully argued by reason of the common good of both society and the souls of men and women. Those who would seek to deny believers their rights as citizens to express their opinions fully and freely in the public square and marketplace of ideas are acting as enemies of democracy. That is the stuff of the secular inquisition and the evil borders of undue "political correctness." We will revisit this issue in chapter 3 on the political "medicating" of citizens.

SEPARATION OF JURISDICTIONS OF GOVERNMENT

Let us also be clear that the Scriptures have given to mankind the mandate of the separation of institutional powers. Governmental power is to be parceled out to the individual, the family, the civil authorities, the marketplace and the institution of the church. These five jurisdictions of government have biblically explicit rights and responsibilities, which I assume most of you, my fellow Christian leaders, know and have versed others on. Tyranny is therefore defined as the usurpation of power or responsibility of one jurisdiction over another.[3] As we will see in chapter 4, this usurpation has been exercised most forcefully over the last centuries by civil government increasingly centralizing its powers and diminishing the rights and responsibilities of the other four jurisdictions.

Therefore, the need to separate the institutions of civil government from the institution of the church is not properly an issue for the church; we are very clear on that reality. Politically speaking, our claim to this demand precedes even the Greek political theorists. The Old Testament Law required this institutional separation of powers and Saul, Israel's first king, was chastised for violating this mandate.[4] What is patently impossible is the separation of spiritual or religious thought from the civil management of society. Secular authoritarianism has a long and deceptive arm when it dons this specious argument, and parades it as being a concept which serves society and protects it from religious encroachments. Who is protecting us from the secularists, especially with the track record of their destructiveness as previously noted?

---

3. 1 Samuel 8:7-18.
4. 1 Samuel 13:7-14.

ON THE RELIGIOUS NATURE OF ALL LAW

Make no mistake; all law is, by its very nature, religious since it defines the nature of both good and evil by its edicts. Law claims some ultimate source from which it draws its moral authority, either generated by man or by some higher power of nature or the Creator thereof. To deny religious expression of thought to the formation of civil law is absurd on its face and conspiratorial by either design or ignorant default. For believers to not commonly know this is an indictment of the leaders of the churches of the world and has caused gross harm to the nations which those church leaders are responsible to disciple. Removing biblical principles from the process and discussion of society's economic management renders the common man a victim to those who most benefit from those principles' absence. The resultant economic system is then free to sidestep the challenges of Christ's supreme commandment which measures the justice and ethics of the system. Injustice tends to gather force around power and money,[5] and that evades the scrutiny of regulation and accountability.

Secularism has historically relied on the "absolutes" of science and rationalism as its source of higher authority and empowerment. However, now that science has shifted away from the absolutism of Newtonian physics and donned the hat of "relativity," and secular rationalism has faltered so spectacularly over the last century, it has birthed "post-modernity"—that reliance is shaky at best. This secular post-modern child is jaded, skeptical, and has little place for either secularism's parenting or religion's claims to eternal realities.

To the mind of this child, all absolute claims are the work of those using words and theories to establish their own power and control over others, by defining the rules of thought and values. Nothing is absolute and all absolute claims are specious attempts to control others, except this claim now being made by the post-modern mind. Welcome to the absurdity of thought and values which have emerged as a result of this thinking and now would relegate all opinions to the realm of the subjective. The claim of objectivity and speaking on behalf of objective truth is, in and of itself, cause to reject the motives of the speaker who

---

5.   1 Timothy 6:10.

would advocate such a thing in this post-modern context. For us believers, however, our God defines Himself as love,[6] not power, in spite of His having set up the rules of the universe.

In conclusion, neither secularism per se nor post-modern thought is the believer's enemy in this context of choice and freedom of thought. Instead, it is an opportunity to speak and think wisely in terms of the tone with which we approach the public conversations of the people. We need not alter our convictions in the slightest but rather, hold them with a greater measure of humility, and recognize how they will be heard by those so damaged by the fruits of secular modernity's track record over the last centuries. As the apostle Paul reminds us, though our faith stands upon the sure Word of God, we do "see through a glass darkly",[7] and what we see is indeed real but not always configured exactly as we say it is in our own current incompleteness. What a wonderful opportunity for the community of faith to grow up into Christ for His sake, for the world's sake and for our own sake! No, secularism and post-modernity are the foils of opposition designed by God to sharpen us and challenge our assertions where they lack the full integrity of the Scriptures.

CHALLENGES OF RELIGIOUS DUALISM WITHIN OUR OWN CAMP

"Dualism" is shorthand for a philosophical view of reality that believes the material world is inferior and transitory, and the "spiritual world of reality", absent of matter (heaven), is the goal of all truly enlightened people. At first blush, this view appears to be true and reasonable. Indeed, we are to focus on the eternal things which transcend so much of this current reality and likewise, we are to live out of our spirits as we pursue spiritual truths in Christ. However, the Scriptures do not give us a "dualistic" view of reality but rather, a unified view of reality commonly called a "wholistic" view.

God created both spirit and matter as the context for eternity and declared it "good."[8] His universe is just that, a unified field of reality tem-

---

6. 1 John 4:16.
7. 1 Corinthians 13:12.
8. Genesis 1:31.

porarily separated due to the Fall of man, awaiting eternal unification and re-creation at the end of this age and the reentry of Christ into His "new heaven and new earth".[9] If material reality is some lower form of God's intentions, then according to this viewpoint Christ's resurrected material body, and ours to come, is some kind of consolation prize for those who missed God's highest. I don't think so. Nancy Pearcey, in her book *Total Truth,* wisely observes this:

> "From the biblical perspective, the problem with Platonic dualism was that it identified the source of chaos and evil with some part of God's creation—namely matter. Creation was divided into two parts: the spiritual (superior, good) and the material (inferior, bad). This stands in clear opposition to the biblical worldview, which teaches that nothing exists from eternity over against God. Matter is not some preexisting stuff with its own independent properties, capable of resisting God's power."
>
> Total Truth, 2008, p. 76

In the Western world, dualistic thought is the child of Plato, and hence its modern re-appearance is often called "neo-Platonism". It also permeates various tenets of Eastern religions as well, where its proponents seek the "nothingness" of material absence. It was alive and well within the early centuries of the church age and was found within sects of the Gnostics. Dualism is today most common in Christianity in various degrees and forms within those who hold strong Dispensationalist beliefs. They often believe that this current world is designed to perish and that God's Kingdom is postponed until some future time (the Millennium); to engage this current world's ills, they believe, beyond simply leading people to Christ, is a diversion at best and satanically inspired at worst. Dualists have also commonly believed that only pastors, Bible teachers, evangelists, and missionaries are capable of truly being "in the ministry". This belief has created a kind of spiritual classism in the Christian world and designated the lower class, comprising the majority of the church, to the more mundane role of non-ministry. The lower class is therefore primarily useful only

---

9.   Psalm 109:26; Isaiah 65:17; 2 Peter 3:13; Revelation 21:1.

to the church as they support the leaders' vision, financial needs, and work which the upper class of the church leaders is performing.

We will be following the implications of this dualistic thread of thought further as we move through this book. Suffice to say for now, as we turn our attention to some of our introductory comments on the present realities of God's Kingdom on earth today, dualism has reduced the army of God's effective workers to a very small percentage of the church's actual numbers. It also explains the relatively paltry amount of biblical exposition by church thinkers, concerning political or economic thought over the last several centuries, at least in the Protestant world, as this next quote by a prominent Catholic exception to this rule reminds us:

> "The theology of culture has always been weakest at the point of economics. Theologians have managed, in the last four hundred years, to update many of their ideas about the meaning of Christianity—in liturgy, hermeneutics, historical studies, sexual ethics, medical ethics, and many other areas. Yet the level of discussion in economics has hardly advanced beyond the principles of the seventeenth century. Its ethics of distribution are those of Aristotle; its theory of the just wage, its attitudes toward capital and interest, and its view of production, invention, and enterprise are really more a part of the ancient and medieval world than of contemporary economics."
>
> Michael Novak, *Democracy and Mediating Structures*, 1980, p. 180

THE STEP-CHILD OF DUALISM: SEPARATING SALVATION FROM OUR ENTRANCE INTO THE KINGDOM OF GOD

> "Giving thanks to the Father, who has qualified us to share in the inheritance of the saints in Light. For He rescued us from the domain of darkness, and transferred us to the kingdom of His beloved Son."
>
> Colossians 1:12-13

> "'Truly, truly, I say to you, unless one is born again, he cannot see the kingdom of God.' 'Truly, truly, I say to you, unless one is born of water and the Spirit he cannot enter into the kingdom of God.'"
>
> John 3:3, 5

The separation of the Gospel of salvation from its supreme context within the Gospel of the Kingdom of God was one of Satan's most ingenious strategies. The moment of our salvation is our spiritual birth and entry as citizens of God's Kingdom, favor, promises, and empowerment. We are then expected to begin our journey into the knowledge of our God and His ways, principles, and transforming power. As current citizens of the Kingdom we have passed from death unto life and begin to change our external environment and spheres of influence as we experience our own internal transformation in Christ.

Separating the Gospel of salvation from the current realities of the Kingdom "neuters" the effect of God's Kingdom in terms of seeing the possibility of change taking place on the earth beyond the personal behavior of saved people. While saved people should indeed make a difference in multiple ways, this false teaching precludes their energies from doing much to disciple the nations socially or structurally, since all of those dimensions of activity are pushed off into either the millennium or the new age of eternity at Christ's return. Hence, the "privatization" of the Gospel is conveniently set in place willingly by these believers, much to the delight of the forces of darkness and those humans inadvertently agreeing with them.

Our current life on earth is our "training gymnasium" for our life in eternity. Our training in personal living and community living now is our training for both kinds of living in eternity, because both will exist there. Seeking the Kingdom on a daily basis is more than simply prayers for Christ's return; it is looking for opportunities to spend ourselves witnessing His life with both our lives and our words, and seeking to deploy our gifts and callings to release redemption into the social institutions for which Christ died.

When we offer up our prayers for the Father's will on earth to come and His will to be done on earth as it is in heaven, we are in fact not simply asking for Christ to hasten His return; we are making ourselves available to be used in the here-and-now to bring a measure of redemption to the nations by bringing it to where we are currently stationed. Because of the fullness of His Kingdom awaits His return, that fact should offer us no excuse to apply the full measure of what is available from God now to others by our faith and His blood, which broke the world system's claims on man and his institutions.

THE KINGDOM OF GOD IS A BRIDGE INTO ETERNITY

The great challenge the world's value-systems and economic systems face today is sustainability. How do we dig ourselves and our societies out of the massive debt and entitlement issues, while at the same time experience sufficient economic growth to maintain consumption and employment rates as well as our essential social systems? On the social values or philosophical side of the equation, how do we unite the generations with transcendent value systems rather than mere power systems?

The great challenge the church faces today is the shift from a self-focused agenda to a Kingdom-focused agenda. In other words, the church must stop seeking to build itself and let Christ do what He said He would do to achieve this, and instead focus itself on seeking first the Kingdom and equipping her people to be Kingdom-focused rather than self-centered and inordinately preoccupied with their own community of faith.[10] That challenge will force the emergence of a new kind of church leader, an apostolic kind of leader whose mission is wholistic and strategic, one whose end-game is training people to release their engiftment well beyond the walls of their church buildings and their own personal well-being.

The great question we all face today as citizens of our nation is: How can we most expeditiously prepare to make a meaningful difference in both the Kingdom of God and the social systems of our respective cultures? As citizens of both our nation and God's Kingdom, and as those who seek to genuinely disciple nations as leaders, we really need guidance. To begin to answer this question we must begin with attempting to

---

10. Matthew 6:33.

elucidate the biblical perspective of how these two worlds fit together. How do the nations of this age fit into God's transcendent Kingdom?

Obviously, I am not going to attempt to respond to Augustine's masterpiece (*The City of God*)[11] in this limited book but rather, I will cite his treatise as the initial foundational discussion in raising the depth of this question. My focus here is to direct our attention more to dealing summarily with the question of how these two different systems (the Kingdom of God and the kingdom of man) are connected, if at all, to eternal social systems. If they were not, then investing time in attempting to inject man's social systems with principles of Kingdom social systems would indeed be an exercise in futility. If eternity's society is some kind of amorphous mass of individuals with no social constructs or systems, then once again, these efforts I am proposing in the discipling of nations are an exercise in building sandcastles in the air. They would be pure speculations and projections of imagination.

My foundational points are simple:

1. God commands us to "disciple" nations or ethnic groups, because the current applications of His Kingdom principles to them have a relationship with eternity. Indeed, we know that the nations are an eternal people grouping and social system.[12] Furthermore, to limit the "discipling of nations" to simply the message of salvation and life in Christ, as essential and foundational as that is, implies God's Kingdom has no social systems. If that were true, it would not be a "Kingdom" since the essence of the very word *kingdom* implies social systems of government and the like. Indeed, I would direct the reader to a multitude of Scriptures like, "And the government will rest on His shoulders;...There shall be no end to the increase of His government...On the throne of David and over His Kingdom."[13] This language, as well as other Old and

---

11. Augustine, *The City of God and Christian Doctrine, vol. 2, A Select Library of Nicene and Post-Nicene Fathers of the Christian Church*, trans. and ed. Philip Schaff and Henry Wace (New York: The Christian Literature Company, 1890).
12. Revelation 21:24-27; 22:1-2.
13. Isaiah 9:6-7.

New Testament language is consistent with the reality of people groups and implicitly social constructs to them, existing as a part of God's eternal order.

2. The Holy Spirit carries within Himself eternity and is our immediate bridge to it in Christ. God's Kingdom can only be revealed, released or "built," however we want to express this, by the agency of the Holy Spirit working through us,[14] since man cannot achieve this action via his own power. That being the case, any Spirit-driven activity a believer engages in has some connection to that which is eternal. Since Christ has commanded us to disciple, only the Holy Spirit working through us can fulfill that command, discipling nations by definition is linked to eternity.

3. God spent significant time with Moses giving us His blueprint for the appropriate social structures for Israel, and by implication for mankind, since "man shall not live on bread alone, but on every word that proceeds out of the mouth of God."[15] For those of us attempting to obey God's command to disciple nations, our fullest information on biblical socio-economic principles and structures is from the Old Testament, while clearly understanding the fulfillment of the law in Christ.

4. As we move into the later chapters of this book and the discussions of economic and policy recommendations, all of it will rest on the presupposition that the relevant biblical principles have some relationship to eternal structures. However modified they may be in Christ's eternal reign over the nations here on the new earth, those called to labor in this area will be gaining eternal insight. We do see through the glass darkly, but we know that eternal people groups and nations exist after the resurrection and the final end of the age. Once again, those categories of individuals gathered as "nations," presupposes the existence of the structures of relationships which permit their ability to be nations in an orderly fashion with defined social roles.

---

14. Romans 14:17.
15. Matthew 4:4; 5:17-19.

THE PHILOSOPHY OF POWER AS THE FOUNDATION
OF KINGDOM-BASED GOVERNMENT

Perhaps the best and most important example of an eternal principle of government invading time deals with the question of its philosophy of power. Simply stated, the philosophy of power of any individual or organization defines its alignment with Christ more clearly than any other organizational or governmental principle. Power is man's most challenging phenomenon.

No other section of Scripture deals with this issue more clearly and with such powerful language as does Philippians 2:1-11:

"Therefore if there is any encouragement in Christ, if there is any consolation of love, if there is any fellowship of the Spirit, if any affection and compassion, [2] make my joy complete by being of the same mind, maintaining the same love, united in spirit, intent on one purpose. [3] Do nothing from selfishness or empty conceit, but with humility of mind regard one another as more important than yourselves; [4] do not *merely* look out for your own personal interests, but also for the interests of others. [5] Have this attitude in yourselves which was also in Christ Jesus, [6] who although He existed in the form of God, did not regard equality with God a thing to be grasped, [7] but emptied Himself, taking the form of a bond-servant, *and* being made in the likeness of men. [8] Being found in appearance as a man, He humbled Himself by becoming obedient to the point of death, even death on a cross. [9] For this reason also, God highly exalted Him, and bestowed on Him the name which is above every name, [10] so that at the name of Jesus EVERY KNEE WILL BOW, of those who are in heaven and on earth and under the earth, [11] and that every tongue will confess that Jesus Christ is Lord, to the glory of God the Father."

Here the apostle Paul unwraps Christ's philosophy of power in ways only the Holy Spirit could initiate. Real power is found in the empowerment of others and release of them into their own God-given ability to fulfill what God has given them to achieve. In this sense, power and true freedom are one and the same. We become what we give away both as individuals and as organizations.

Freedom and power, then, are found in the principle of the Cross: the others' good at My (Christ's) expense.[16] To have power over others is to take responsibility for giving them the possibility of fulfilling their roles in the group, out of their own internal and freely given engagement of their resources to that end. I am not free until the motivation for obedience is generated internally without external demand. This is what Christ modeled perfectly as prophetically proclaimed by Him in Psalm 40:7-8:

> "Then I said, 'Behold, I come; In the scroll of the book
> it is written of me. I delight to do Your will, O my God;
> Your Law is within my heart.'"

Therefore, taking someone into freedom through our position of power is to open to them the path of the Cross with its attendant disciplines of skills, stewardship, problem solving, and a serious list of other self-governing challenges. True freedom rests upon the platform of character. Please take note of this reality when we discuss how to achieve economic freedom and prosperity for the greatest number of people. It requires a system of power that offers people the pathway to economic prosperity through the gateway of character formation. It similarly challenges the systems of government and the corporate world to create management systems that guide people into concern for the freedom of others. Yes, we are back once more at Christ's greatest commandment, to love others as ourselves, as the foundation of both personal and corporate values and power.

In summary, then, as the Kingdom of God is injected into present reality, it is an injection of a bridge into the eternal and presents a measured foretaste of what eternity feels like. It truly is a "salt" that both preserves and seasons this current world with eternity's flavors. It truly is an extension of "light" that provides clarity of action and the illumination of the hearts of people and the values of organizations. When the church withholds salt and light from people, organizations, or national structures and policies, it is failing to act as the present world's immune system, designed to keep it as healthy as is possible

---

16. John 17.

for the sake of God's purposes.[17] In this life, we are not to be the world's judge but rather its teacher, the one who models what the Scriptures give to mankind as the path to life and prosperity. God's Kingdom is to be the backbone of our lives and the communities we call our church.

THE EMERGING GREAT DEBATE AND OUR ROLE IN IT

Intense political debate is no stranger to the democracies of the world. To some degree they thrive on it, as it injects intense energy into the system and activates the citizens' interest and participation. What will characterize the coming "great debate" will most likely be the intensity of it (commensurate with severe changes to any system), the length of it (due to the massive amounts of money required to resolve its core problems), and the ideological entrenchments of those who are polarized on opposite borders of the issues.

Without Christ's values being effectively posited into any political-economic system, it will increasingly self-destruct and destroy many of its own people and the other systems dependent on it. As stated already, the church is designed to be the immune system of the nations. There, the love of Christ and love of our fellow man demand our wise and effective involvement. Christ did not remove the possibility of poverty, exploitation, death, and entropy. What He did do is affirm God's principles of life, freedom, prosperity, and choice for all men, women, and systems that align themselves with those principles. But unless we are present in this great debate in the communities in which we live and interact, where will people hear these things? I trust we are not expecting the masses to come on Sunday and hear them in most of our churches. No, as citizens of our nations we must take these principles to the streets, so to speak.[18]

This great debate must, and I believe will, force a level of strategic planning into the political process largely absent now in most nations. Because economic growth and political stability secure a nation,

----

17. 1 Timothy 2:1-4.
18. Proverbs 1:20-21.

and because economics supplies the basic needs of people and their expectations for the lives of their children as well, this debate will eventually mobilize unprecedented numbers of voters. We will begin to hear cries for national energy strategies, defense strategies, secured borders, value-based citizenship training in public schools, essential industry programs, water systems, and a whole host of other national strategic programs.

One might say that we hear this outcry already. Yes, but its intensity is going to go far beyond what we have heard in the past. Why? Because of the increasingly interactive global economy and the increasing challenges of global labor competition, not just production competition. Modern trade and global competition have surely "flattened" the world as many are saying.

Technology is constantly reducing production costs and creating efficiencies that raise international labor pool demands in ways unheard of in history. This increased competition will put stress on the need for internal national consumption rates like nothing we have ever seen. Many nations can now significantly out-produce what they can either successfully export or internally consume at globally competitive prices (China comes to mind). This makes the need to grow (internal middle-class consumption rates) go through the roof. But I am getting ahead of myself. My point is this: We have never been here before and while the debt and entitlement issues are front and center, resolving them alone will not resolve a set of other problems like the ones just mentioned. The net of all this is that the great debate is going to carry the energy of millions and millions of people who no longer have a guarantee of a stable or certain lifestyle which they may have experienced up to this point in their lives. We do not know for sure what form of release this energy may take.

The most difficult part of this current phase of the economic situation is the growing tensions between the hope of creating balanced civil budgets and the servicing of current debt obligations, as weighed against the maintenance of social entitlement programs. Math cannot change the realities of this conflict; it can only make them all the more jagged and unflinching. The Western nations of the world have almost without exception promised a collective social lifestyle that cannot be paid for in either the short run or the long run. As we will forcefully discuss in the closing chapter of this book, this opens and "forces" the church into both a huge opportunity to reshape itself or further isolate itself as a socially irrelevant force in the cultures in which it resides. Love for someone demands relevancy; to be perceived as irrelevant is to be shut out as uncaring.

LET'S FISH FOR MEN AND WOMEN THROUGHOUT THE WORLD

"'Follow Me, and I will make you fishers of men.'"
Matthew 4:19

You catch fish, as a rule, by fishing with bait that looks like what they are used to feeding on. We should not expect to catch fish in the sporting goods store either. We must go out to where the fish are and wisely engage them there with their most frequently used foods. So it is with fishing for men; we must engage them in ways and in places where they are most comfortable, while discussing the things they usually talk about before we attempt to move things toward our own agendas.[19] So what are they most frequently discussing? In the main, it is jobs, hobbies, relationships, and the daily concerns of life. Just like fish, if abnormal things are introduced to them they frequently draw back and retreat.

The world of common people is in a conversation that publicly centers on current events and the general issues affecting their common needs and concerns. Religious or spiritual issues do come up, but as a rule the general public in the secular society has been socially pressured by the secularists to attempt to keep religion a "private matter", leaving it behind when we are discussing the management of public concerns and public policies. This requires, then, that we become skilled at knowing how to turn a conversation toward the possibility of spiritual values actually being very relevant to current social issues, and indeed carrying the possibility of resolving many current social challenges. Many people are increasingly open to a values-driven conversation

---

19. Matthew 11:19; Mark 2:16.

and what is happening as a result of the absence of the discussion of values in modern culture.

The challenge is commonly this: Where and how are most Christians going to become equipped to engage in such conversations over public policy issues and the spiritual principles that should be applied to them? They seldom will be equipped like that in church. While there are some excellent groups doing that kind of equipping through so-called "para-church" organizations, we need many, many more both churches and para-church groups doing this to prepare believers. Jesus is the perfect example of someone taking the perceived interest of those He encountered and gently turning them toward the core spiritual issues behind them or related to them. Having access to the Holy Spirit, and the possibility of pursuing more personal education in these areas, we should all be making a concerted effort to become particularly well versed in some area of these public issues. Relevance requires preparation.

Before we leave this issue of our need to get into the public conversation more deeply and on a much wider scale, let me make some further observations:

1. We need to bring principles, not politics, to the process. Criticizing the political parties and their shortcomings puts us on the wrong foot. Principles are far more important than personalities or political parties. Take the high ground in any fight, if possible. There are already too many critics and not enough problem solvers.

2. Stick to one or two issues at the most. If the people who you encounter can comfortably handle more than that, they are likely to make you look silly unless you are ready for a more strategic conversation with a well prepared opponent. If you are, go for it.

3. This economic reset is going to be a "war of attrition" so to speak. It will likely go on for the next decade, due to the size and complexity of the problems and challenges that politicians will face to finally come to agreement on the way out of these issues. After they do agree they must have the willingness to enact these really hard policies and then garner the support of the people.

I hope that the process will be shorter. However, with the lack of education among citizens, in terms of understanding the root issues surrounding these problems, and the further complication of electing unprepared leaders, it could easily go on for a prolonged time. It is very clear that the churches must put on a major concerted effort into rapidly widening and deepening the preparations of their people to properly engage this historic opportunity and challenge.

THIS ECONOMIC CRISIS WILL ROLL OUT IN THREE PHASES

I expect this current crisis to continue to roll out in three generally distinct phases. Each phase will demand coming to the reality that there is no way out of this crisis—there is only a path through it. It is not going to go away, although it will have intermittent short periods of hope only to be pulled back down into the jaws of the dilemma, replete with unfunded obligations, shrinking revenues, unmet social needs, and plenty of angry people.

PHASE ONE:
ECONOMIC STAGNATION, DENIAL,
AND TOTALLY INSUFFICIENT REMEDIES

"In a calm sea, every man is a captain."

Ernest Hemingway

Phase One became public in September 2008 as the housing bubble popped, financial institutions faced failure, and the less publicaly known derivatives market obligations threatened to sink the global financial markets. Obviously all of these things were building up prior to their unveiling.

As is commonly known now, the initial reaction of the general public was surprise, then concern, and then a degree of denial that things could really be as serious as some were saying. They truly had no idea how close we were to a global meltdown. Then came the bailouts, as government money pumped significant funds into the system. This was done for cosmetic appearances, as well as for specific needs, since large portions of the funds appropriated were never dispersed or dispersed in ways not directly related to the stated areas of acute financial need in order to "save the system." Seven hundred billion dollars were allocated and only some 400 billion dollars were spent. One hundred and thirty-three billion dollars is still owed to the government and much of it is unlikely to be repaid.

Since the public dimensions of Phase One we have seen a prolonged stagnation of the economy; prolonged levels of high unemployment, rivaling the Great Depression levels in certain areas of the United States; major financial challenges to the European Union as member countries continue to reveal their near insolvency and require their own bailouts; and growing anxiety as the public is told of the increasing size of the financial challenges. What now stands in front of us in the closing time period of Phase One are the political shifts yet to take place in global elections and the legislative and executive branch "remedies" coming from those elections. We are also holding our breath relative to the EU crisis and its further effect on markets, as nations continue to have their bond ratings lowered and therefore interest rates are increased. This will likely take us several more years to muddle through.

PHASE TWO:
THE BRIDGE PERIOD BETWEEN OLD AND NEW NORMAL

"Some people feel that because they are Christians they are immune from the catastrophes of life. Not so. Hear Jesus as He prays for His Disciples, and for us: 'I pray not that thou shouldest take them out of the world, but that thou shouldest keep them from the evil one....sanctify (or mature) them through thy truth: thy word is truth'"

John 17:15, 17

"These Bylaws of the Kingdom are His Word—His truth. Through the obeying of them, we shall be kept—not from the calamities necessarily—but from the evil one who would delight to see our house tumble all around us when the winds of adversity begin to blow....Those less fortunate

> than we may look to us for preservation and illumination
> when darkness and the storms of life descend."
>
> Bob Mumford, *The King and You*, 1974, p. 242

The length of Phase Two, which I believe we will enter sometime after the next rounds of elections and governments have proposed and enacted their next set of policies, will be directly determined by the willingness of these government actions to realistically address the core issues of the crisis, rather than kicking the can down the street and crossing their fingers. I am not currently holding my breath and hoping for the best. The cost cutting or spending increases will largely be determined by both economic philosophy and perceived public demands, both of which can be based on ignorance, denial, and political expediency.

Phase Two will be the most dangerous period for sure. The masses of the baby boomers will engulf our already bankrupt social systems here in the U.S. It remains to be seen how much truth the public can bear and if the politicians can actually enact appropriate remedies. We will desperately need true statesmen and stateswomen who can elevate themselves to the required level of courage, to do what should be done for the good of the whole and stand the forthcoming heat from special interest groups among all sectors of society used to feeding off the benefits of the old systems. To my economist friends, we will soon see which school of thought will carry the day: Cambridge or Chicago?

The reemergence of the importance of the family unit will certainly be a very significant phenomenon. During the last Great Depression, people went home. Today many dislocated souls have no family to go home to. As an institution, the family has been severely emaciated since the 1930s. We will also discuss this issue in chapter 5 as we discuss the economic power of generational momentum. Suffice to say for now, the decrease in social funding and commensurate power shifts away from reliance on centralized government funding will continue to put extreme pressure on local governments and communities. This is where Phase Two will make itself felt most acutely on the local level.

This is also where the church must step up and show up, as we will later see.

Between now and then we will continue to see increased tensions between unionized sectors of employment and non-union workers; between public service workers and private sector workers, over glaring wage discrepancies; between ethnic groups, over differing levels of unemployment; between those in the extreme upper levels of income and those wanting to see them defunded or at least see the removal of their absurd tax loopholes so publicly decried. Tensions will exist also as more nations seek capital infusions from other stronger nations; both the EU and the U.S. will have greater challenges in securing needed financing from other national sources. Here in the U.S., the baby boomers' demographic "hit" to social systems will begin to numerically peak over the next decade, further collapsing existing systems. Global currency systems will most likely change, as fiat money becomes no longer trusted. The list could go on. This is not the end of the world but it surely is a major shift in the way the world will do business.

PHASE THREE: THE NEW NORMAL

I personally do not expect Christ's return to be right around the corner. The church is too far from being ready to graduate to its next eternal assignment and it has surely not discipled the nations or sufficiently modeled the Kingdom of God as a witness to the world.[20] Nevertheless, the world will have had to face up to a set of realities that moved it closer to sustainable models of social structuring, and society will have had to face up to the consequences of rejecting many of its historic spiritual roots. Phase Three will begin the journey of living out the consequent changes it has had to make to reorder its economic and political philosophies concerning the roles of its citizens and the functional abilities of civil government to support them. Local communities will not soon give up their newfound powers after having fought their battles to achieve power and survive. The resulting civil decentralization from this crisis will not be so easily reversed, as it was in the twentieth century when the emergence of the modern state

---

20. Matthew 24:14.

increasingly disempowered smaller units of society. Local communities will once again have significant political powers.

So on we go, to look at the phenomena of "the medicating of the citizens," in terms of the social and economic systems and some of the challenges this has given us. As we leave behind the issues of dualism and the secular inevitabilities of dissent in a choice-based political system, may we take away the most critical point being made here for those of us who identify with Christ and His Kingdom. We have the privilege of altering history as a result of this crisis. We must seize it wisely and both model and assert the mandate of Christ's greatest commandment. The current economic Darwinism in any form is toxic, social systems without spiritual values are transitory, and apathetic or untrained Christianity is complicit with any of these secular outcomes.

CHAPTER 3

THE TWILIGHT OF FREEDOM IN THE WEST

The only truly legitimate goal of all government is the physical protection of its citizens' lives, property, and civil rights, and the empowerment and strengthening of their capacities for self-government and freedom under God.[1] This is the standard by which enlightened leaders should measure their own goals and performance. If freedom is the ability to obey God, then love is the desire and extension of that right to all others. It is painful beyond words to describe how far short our current world governments are from missing that standard and how quickly many of them are moving in the opposite direction. Unfortunately, my nation is among them.

The United States and other nations are "medicating" their citizens with an assortment of "narcotics" as habit-forming and mind numbing as any of the illegal drugs their governments seek to outlaw. These medications are covert, touted as universally acceptable by the majority of citizens, and gradually destroying the possibility of producing clear thinking, self-governing citizens capable of producing sustainable social systems or economically viable nations. Among these drugs are the public educational systems which focus on self-approbation instead of the capacity to reason clearly and become lifelong learners, entertainment and cultural art which constantly elevates the basest of human behavior, and the singling out of Judeo-Christian principles

---

1. Romans 13:1-7.

and morals for their eradication in as many ways as is possible in the context of allegedly free democratic societies. In this chapter we will examine these issues.

Before we delve deeper into these assertions we must comment once again on one of the major premises of this book: This current social and economic crisis is going to be used of God to refocus believers on His Kingdom, on seeking it first as He commanded, and the practical ways in which this crisis is tailor-made for that endeavor. The Kingdom of God, as a social discussion point, is relatively new territory for most people living today, both Christian and non-believers. Therefore, few walls of "protection" by society have been prejudicially built up against it, as they currently exist against "Christianity", being "born again", or pronouncements of "let me tell you about my church and what Jesus has done for me." God is going to use this crisis to both enhance His people's value in the minds of the unbelievers and redirect the church to the equipping of its people to evangelize out of their social context and not just within their own lives—to learn to "net fish" socially and not be limited just to pole-fishing on an individual, one-on-one basis.

PREACHING CHRIST AND HIS KINGDOM: RESIDENT ALIENS

"'Again, the kingdom of heaven is like a dragnet cast into the sea, and gathering fish of every kind; and when it was filled, they drew it upon the beach; and they sat down, and gathered the good fish into the containers, but the bad they threw away. So it will be at the end of the age; the angels shall come forth, and take out the wicked from among the righteous, and throw them into the furnace of fire;'"
Matthew 13:47-50

Matthew 13 is the chapter in the New Testament wherein Jesus teaches His disciples most repeatedly on the nature of the Kingdom of God. In this particular parable He tells His disciples that prior to His return, His Kingdom will be gathering people throughout the nations of the world (virtually all Bible scholars agree on this interpretation), and that within the "net" of the Kingdom there will be "good" and "wicked" fish. Obviously, the good fish are those to whom Christ's salvation has been imparted and received, and the wicked are those whose rejection of their redemption leaves them with a fatally flawed human nature, which will not allow them into the presence of God and His eternal Kingdom. What far too many believers seem to miss is the fact that Jesus is teaching here that His Kingdom, in this pre-eternal Kingdom dispensation, will have fellow travelers who are not His subjects, or more specifically, members of His church.

Indeed, His Kingdom is now open to those fellow travelers of Christ who seek to live by some of His principles and derive the benefits of so doing, without fully accepting His salvation or Lordship personally. Many have seen the reality that everyone who goes to church or proclaims themselves to be a "Christian", isn't. To see that is commendable. To see that the preaching of His Kingdom truths and lifestyle offers a genuine alternative possibility rather than simply inviting people into the church as we know it opens a whole new realm of possibilities. I am not saying we should preach or teach the Gospel any differently than the apostle Paul, for example. What I am saying is that preaching Christ and His Kingdom, like Jesus did, rather than Christ and His church, offers an unexplored venue to people who live in a world largely turned off by the church and seldom if ever exposed to the concept of His Kingdom.

My personal experience all over the world is that most people are fascinated by a discussion of Christ's Kingdom, and are often cautious or even hostile to a discussion inviting them on a pathway into His church. I have spent my adult life serving the church and attempting to serve and equip her people, but I also recognize that Jesus will build His church most completely if we present and demonstrate His Kingdom.[2] The point of this is that nations can be turned towards Kingdom truths that pragmatically work in whole areas of government and social structures. This is social "net fishing", presenting Kingdom truths and principles relative to a nation's social structures and their viability and not simply the people's personal lives. This offers believers evangelistic opportunities and possibilities to disciple whole nations, offering people groups and citizens the social and economic

---

2. Matthew 16:18-19.

fruits of God's Kingdom as proofs of His reality and love for them.[3] This will encourage them to see that if God's truths work socially, then they may work personally as well. That kind of thinking is the desired outcome of our work. It will open many of their eyes and pull them into His Kingdom net, thereby giving them a clearer perspective of Christ as Savior on a personal level.

Because many of our social systems are failing, political parties are vying for the hearts and votes of the disenchanted. So should we. Political parties will not give people the kind of spiritual foundation to make truly wise, political decisions because they are currently prohibited by social pressures from doing so. In order for us to do so, however, we must vastly upgrade the kind of information being given to believers dealing with the biblical principles of political structures, economic policies, and strategies to make them more relevant in our modern social contexts. As noted in the last chapter, the secular world has prejudicially painted the vast majority of believers as fools or social retards afraid to deal with either advanced reasoning or the effects of social "progress." Unfortunately, some of these charges against us are true but the responsibility for this must first rest upon our leaders. We have not trained them as well equipped citizens, capable and active in their abilities to discuss social issues from a biblical perspective.

Indeed, getting into the world's conversation is a significant part of our strategy; as society gets weaker, the secularists become more desperate and the church's leaders are better equipped to train their people, the "table is being set" for those of us who are hungry to see Christ exalted and His Kingdom expanded. We therefore welcome the growing great debate within the cultures of the world.

As the three-phased crisis continues to roll out, and the politicians' "answers" remain insufficient to deal with the true depth of our global challenges, a growing frustration and fear will continue to rise in the people. The real answers to problems will require leaders who deal in truth, not politics and simply short-term expedient needs, or primarily catering to special interest groups. We need leaders who are clear on

---

3.   2 Chronicles 9:5-8.

the price tag that goes with where we are, and are willing to pay the price to help lead us out.

Here in the United States there are millions of Christians who are not "Kingdom conscious," so to speak. They are unaware of the eternal value to be learned by believers as they give themselves to the task of building community and thinking through the social structures that promote freedom and life. There are also a growing number of "undecided and disillusioned" citizens who are losing faith in the system. These are the habitats of resident aliens for God's Kingdom, awaiting the emergence of Christian leaders who are clear enough on the principles of freedom in the context of democratic pluralism to be trusted both by God and man to pull large numbers of people together and take us into the next phase of our Father's plan for the earth. It is of note that Israel too had its "resident aliens", who in Solomon's time, counting women and children would have numbered nearly a million people.[4] Similar, unique conditions for the further release of God's Kingdom exist in many other nations. God is waiting to release to His leaders the strategies to properly respond to them.

If enough believers could focus on leading people to truth, rather than focusing on leading them into their particular church, I have confidence that the Holy Spirit can lead them to Christ and Christ can lead them into His Church Himself. This kind of faith is a stretch for many believers now, but as God leads His people further into this crisis I strongly suspect that many of our paradigms will be both stretched and rearranged. A Kingdom-focused church seeks to build up people for Christ's Kingdom, not their own. Sufficient pressure is coming to produce many, many more of these kinds of churches.

SPIRITUAL FORCES UNDERGIRDING
NATIONAL IDEOLOGIES AND SOCIAL SYSTEMS

"For our struggle is not against flesh and blood, but against rulers, against the powers, against the world forces of this darkness, against the spiritual forces of wickedness in the heavenly places."
Ephesians 6:12

---

4.   2 Chronicles 2:17.

At the Fall of man, Adam and Eve lost for humanity the spiritual control over the earth. God obviously kept the power to trump Satan's newfound control over the earth's spiritual atmosphere,[5] but Scripture clearly indicates that Satan and his assigned senior minions took firm control over the "second heavens" and the emerging social and ideological systems of people groups and nations. While we will deal with these issues more thoroughly in chapter 9, as we discuss the discipling of nations and the strand of the threefold cord of compelling prayer, we must comment on them briefly now as well.

Obviously, the secular world does not believe in or understand the orderly ways in which God has set up the "rules of the game," let alone the demonic hierarchies He has allowed to oversee both cultures and geographical settings. The secularists think we are crazy and primitive, while we realize that they actually believe that all of man's thinking comes from himself and that he is not truly influenced by any spiritual beings.[6] As we were all taught at the universities, such "spiritual" ideas are powerful superstitions, which operate in the realm of self-imposed unrealities at best, or schizophrenic tendencies at worst. My point here is this: the ideologies and spiritual "climates" we face in our culture are undergirded and "glued in place," so to speak, by these rebellious spiritual forces. They cannot be displaced by merely the power of sound and reasonable arguments or the simple eloquence of an excellent speaker.

This means we are fighting the "medicating of citizens" on two different levels, one spiritual and invisible and the other one cultural and coming through human beings. On the "underside" of things we are dealing with these rebellious spirits with the power of prayer and the declarative authority of the local *ecclesiae,* which we will delve deeply into in chapter 9. On the "top" side of things, we are dealing publicly with the ideologies of cultures and nations and their public policy structures and systems, by using sound biblical reasoning and the anointing of the Holy Spirit upon people called to function in this social realm.[7] We are fulfilling Paul's admonition to walk out the realities of these Scriptures:

---

5. 2 Corinthians 4:4; Ephesians 2:2; Colossians 2:15-23.
6. 1 Corinthians 2:14.
7. 1 Corinthians 2:4.

> "For though we walk in the flesh, we do not war according
> to the flesh, for the weapons of our warfare are not of the
> flesh, but divinely powerful for the destruction of fortresses.
> We are destroying speculations and every lofty thing raised
> up against the knowledge of God, and we are taking every
> thought captive to the obedience of Christ."
>
> 2 Corinthians 10:3-5

This is precisely what the apostle Paul is telling Christians to do, fight the spiritual forces undergirding the intellectual thought processes of the cultures in which you find yourselves. The war is being waged on both levels, by the forces of Satan and the fallen thinking of man, and we must therefore fight the war for the minds and souls of man on both levels. This calls for a division of labor on behalf of the saints, wherein the believers know who they are and their resident gifts in Christ, and deploy them accordingly. We will fight the enemies of freedom in the spiritual realm and fight them publicly with the reasoned logic of anointed Kingdom truths.

Fallen man is driven by three corrupting forces:[8] the sensual lusts of the flesh and eyes; the intellectual pride of life undergirded by the drive for power; and the effects of the unseen spiritual forces working against him, which are designed to pollute him and keep him outside of God's eternal Kingdom. Therefore, as we will now see, the medicating of the citizens and subsequent loss of freedom is being administered to each of these three cultural vulnerabilities.

THE MEDICATED CITIZEN: DECEIVED MINDS, DRUG-LIKE CURRENT ENTERTAINMENT, AND THE POISON OF CULTURALLY APPROVED RELIGION

Neil Postman's book *Amusing Ourselves to Death,* and Allan Bloom's book *The Closing of the American Mind,* are but two of the better books released over the last decades dealing with the challenges of the

---

8. 1 John 2:16.

"medicating" of citizens in modern society.[9] I am not offering some new theory of the dumbing down and numbing down of modern man by the dual forces of spiritual beings and fallen humanity. What I am saying is that until church leaders begin to broaden their sermons to apply biblical truths to contemporary issues, and enlighten their followers how to protect themselves and then go on the offensive to liberate others, our surrounding cultures will continue to suffer the effects of these mind-altering and soul-killing narcotics. My fellow leaders and believers, we really are the world systems' immune system and our failure to do these things in our pulpits and churches has made us complicit in the destruction of our nations. Until we see this and repent en masse, we will be fighting a guerrilla war rather than running a strategic command operation.

Our culture's entertainment products are driven to appeal to society's lowest common denominators, corrupting our youth and injecting them with delusions of grandeur concerning the long-term value of their season of life and the superficiality of many of their values. These products also feed the animosities of the radical Moslems who cannot understand how nations that are allegedly built upon the Scriptures can be purveyors of such pollution. It reinforces the hold-out Marxists who rightly perceive the consumption-driven motives behind much of this drivel, and has made being "cool" the standard by which the most recent generations judge the veracity of later generations. Do we honestly wonder why and how our economic and political debacles came about when we are producing and exporting this poisonous drivel. Craig M. Gay's quote is particularly painful and relevant:

> "...the modern system is founded upon the repudiation of Jesus' assertion that man does not live by bread alone. On the contrary, the moderns retort, man lives quite well by bread alone so long as he can be distracted—by means

9. Neil Postman, *Amusing Ourselves to Death: Public Discourse in the Age of Show Business* (New York: Viking, 1985); Allan Bloom, *The Closing of the American Mind: How Higher Education Has Failed Democracy and Impoverished the Souls of Today's Students* (New York: Simon and Schuster, 1987).

of entertainment and therapy—from asking imponderable religious questions."

Craig M. Gay, Cash Values: Money and the Erosion of Meaning in Today's Society, 2003, p. 50

Our media and arts offerings are all too often of the same ilk: crass, simplistic, and geared to fit the endless stream of ill-educated youth we continue to press out of our so-called public education systems.[10] Our focus is on feeling good about ourselves, when we ought to be getting the signal that the reason we need to do so is at an all-time high because we are creating valueless deserts in our cultures. We should be feeling *bad* about ourselves; we have earned it.

Could these phenomena in any way be related to the paucity of sermons going out over our pulpits, which encourage believers to consider deeply repenting for our shortcomings? In the current church, especially the "new wave" churches, there is one supreme rule: make sure the people leave feeling good about themselves and how much God loves them just as they are. The culture has deeply evangelized us, and we have come to believe that the culture's "medicine" is the best way to persuade people to become disciples of Christ. Isn't Jesus nice? Let's all feel warm and fuzzy now.

People are medicated for the following reasons: 1) the medication will help heal them or relieve pain, 2) they need medication to prepare for a medical procedure, 3) the medication will allow someone else to control them, or 4) they medicate themselves for reasons of escape or excitement. Today's citizens are being medicated for reasons three and four: 3) control by those wanting power or because they believe that certain groups of citizens are incompetent to care for themselves, and 4) self-medication because the pain of life is seemingly too much for some people to bear. This patronizing medication of citizens is all about racism, classism, leaders' need for power to enhance their financial positions, or leaders' simple arrogance and ignorance—having no clue as to how to truly lead or love people. Our citizens don't need

---

10. Isaiah 3:4-5.

medicating. They need the skill set to think clearly and the character to be legitimately self-reliant and self-governing.[11]

So many of our social entitlement programs are related to these fundamental issues we are now discussing. We are defunding these programs because of our cruelty and the unabated misuse of power in societies that are committed to keeping citizens ignorant of the very principles that would lead to their freedom. Private and public education are among the first duties of the church, but shame on us Christians because we should know that and be acting upon it. Indeed, education is the primary way to disciple a nation. What is happening in society reflects our "no show" status.

So what shall we further say about the secular religion currently being approved by our leaders, which they say is designed to keep people safe from religious intrusions into the public square or the inciting of divisions amongst the people? Didn't we already take a short look at leaders' track records concerning their benign protection in an earlier chapter? Yes, we did and it was not pretty. Have they wrecked the train and helped divide the people, or has it been the church? As noted already, the wreckage has been due to their leadership underwritten by the church's failure to be the salty and light- driven social institution God designed us to be. We have both failed.

ON THE NATURE OF TRULY FREE CITIZENS

Citizens are free only when they recognize clearly how easily freedom is lost and how difficult it can be to recover it. That evident reality creates diligent hearts fastened and focused, firstly on our responsibilities as citizens and secondly on our rights and the rights of others. May God have mercy on us for how far away from this reality many presently are. In the Western world we have largely become nations of "rights", filled with citizens for whom their governments have the onus of responsibilities, and only incidentally the citizens.

Permit me to outline my comments on this critical subject of creating a free citizenry using seven principal points. This subject has filled many

---

11. 2 Timothy 1:7, KJV.

books and my insights shall be brief for the sake of the larger intents of this study. Each of these seven points has economic consequences. We shall also see this more fully as we examine them and move into more explicit chapters dealing directly with economic realities and their connections with political or philosophical concepts.

All social and political ignorance costs money because it is inefficient and often destructive. Ignorance creates unending social programs that attempt to deal with its consequences. Social ignorance drains the citizens of their resources and eventually destroys their economic initiative and desire to invest in people or projects. What now follows are some Kingdom remedies to political ignorance and economic poverty.

1. Free citizens think and are trained to think both biblically and therefore principally. Here are some examples of principled thinking in the political realm, or jurisdiction of civil government:

    a. Political freedom is not free; it costs many people a great deal to achieve it and it will take many people to sacrificially hold on to it.

    b. Self-government is the foundation of a truly free citizenry; as a rule, the more that self-government exists in a nation, the less new external laws are required to govern people.[12]

    c. Nations require a clearly written constitution that is fully endorsed by the majority of citizens to govern across the generations. The principal values of a constitution must be studied by every generation and all new foreign immigrants seeking citizenship, if those values are to stay operable and the people united in their view of the transcendent principles which take precedence over their own personal preferences.

    d. Centralization has limits for its efficiencies (the law of diminishing returns), and bureaucracy tends to grow far beyond those limits. Centralization must constantly be

---

12. Hebrews 10:16.

held in check by directing power and responsibility back to the local communities and their citizens.

e. Nations must not shield their citizens from the consequences of their own bad decisions unless they are being trained and committed to not repeating them. This principle has major economic consequences.[13]

The lists could go on and on. The major point is this: The ineffective politicians currently being elected by our ignorant electorate tells us that whatever freedom or transcendent principles were governing us, no longer are doing so now.

2. Free citizens understand that whoever controls the education of children controls the future of their nation. Nations which turn the education of their children over to the civil government, without parental control of that educational system, are casting off control of their nations' future. From a biblical perspective, parents have primary responsibility for their children and parents may well turn portions of their children's education over to whoever they wish, but the "tutors" (school systems) should not have control over the values and thinking processes of those children.[14] When that happens, the state is now the surrogate parent and will inevitably become the legal parent.

3. The state (civil government) cannot control the thoughts of its citizens nor their basic rights of free speech, assembly, religious freedom, and the other fundamental rights carefully document-ed in their constitutions. The U.S. Constitution is an incredible document and should be followed by our courts, not "updated" to reflect judges' values. Its core presuppostion is that man is given his rights by God and not the state (our Declaration of Independence). There are multiple leaders, educators, lawyers, and politicians who no longer believe this and tacitly function as if the state is the source of all political rights. Now, in the United States, Christianity is being tolerated as a "private faith", by in-

13. Jeremiah 6:14.
14. Galatians 4:1-2.

creasingly denying its ability to influence the secular systems of our nation. Jesus' greatest commandment begins, "love God." He is the source of your inherent liberties. Historically, when man's civil government has no appeal to transcendent principles, tyranny takes over and then the eventual overthrow of that tyranny occurs.

4. God gave man, through Judeo-Christianity, protection from his own fallen tendencies to abuse power. God gave us a biblical blueprint for a system of separated political powers that is unrivaled by any other major religion in the world. It is called "jurisdictional government" by some, or "sphere sovereignty" by others. Political scientists have called it the "doctrine of separated powers". The Scriptures teach that there are essentially four spheres of government: 1) self-government, 2) family government, 3) ecclesiastical government, and 4) civil government. A fifth sphere has been noted by many as the sphere of modern business, necessitated by the creation of the legal "persons" called corporations, which thereupon took the field of commerce out of its historical place as an extension of family-related commerce and gave it its own sphere of government.

Each sphere of government is given responsibilities and guidelines in terms of relating to each other.[15] "Tyranny" is defined as the usurpation of power by one sphere of government over another. Modern tyranny has most predominantly taken place by civil government as it extended its claims of governing power over all other spheres, and hence the

15. Dennis Peacocke, Winning the Battle for the Minds of Men (Santa Rosa: Strategic Christian Services, 1987), 18-19. See also: Proverbs 16:32; 25:28; Luke 9:23; Acts 24:25; 1 Corinthians 9:25; 2 Corinthians 10:5; Galatians 5:22-24; 2 Timothy 1:7; Hebrews 12:11; 2 Peter 2:9-19; Genesis 2:18; 3:16; Deuteronomy 6:1-9; Ephesians 5:21-31; Colossians 3:18; Matthew 18:18-20; 22:21; 1 Timothy 3:1-15; 5:17-22; Titus 1:6-9; 1 Thessalonians 5:17; Hebrews 13:7-17; 1 Peter 5:1-5; Exodus 20:15-17; Numbers 27:1-9; Deuteronomy 8:17-18; 28:1-18; Proverbs 6:1-5; 10:2; 11:4; 13:22; 15:16; 23:4-5; Philippians 4:19; Hebrews 7:4-10; 1 Corinthians 9:6; Exodus 18:19-23; Deuteronomy 1:13-17; 2 Samuel 23:3-4; Psalm 2:10-12; 33:12; Proverbs 8:12-16; 11:11; 14:34; 29:12; Isaiah 10:1; Romans 13:1-7; 1 Timothy 1:8-10; Luke 19:21-23; Matthew 28:18-20; Romans 14:17.

state has become "god," as the German philosopher Hegel delightedly once proclaimed. The separation of powers view of civil government was clearly reinforced during the Reformation, and underpinned the founding documents of the United States. This marriage between the Christian view of government and the extension of its legal system was so strong that, until the second half of the 1800s, the lawyers and seminarians here in the U.S. commonly studied the first five books of the Bible (the Pentateuch) together because of their common heritage. Civil law, at this point in time, was predominantly based on the biblical civil laws of the Old Testament. William Blackstone's *Commentaries on the Laws of England,* our seminal textbook on English law, went back and forth between his study of legal principles and their grounding in the Scriptures.

What is economically significant about this is that once one sees the reality of the separated powers of government, the question then arises: Which jurisdiction is responsible for the financing of particular obligations of public finance? This is called "jurisdictional financing" or "jurisdictional problem-solving", and we will deal with it in upcoming chapters as an essential skill set in the governing of nations and the establishment of their taxation policies and fiscal policies. Who indeed is responsible to pay for what our governments are doing? Which jurisdictions—the individual, the family, the church, the commercial sphere, or the civil government—are financially responsible for specific elements of public priorities and their costs?

5. The free citizen and the free nation are governed not by the principle of "survival of the fittest" or the "power of enlightened self-interest", but rather by Christ's Kingdom principle of being grounded in God's love for us and His creation, and loving others with an extension of that same love. As we will soon see in our unfolding discussions regarding economic principles of sustainable prosperity for the greatest number of people, our systems of capital creation must likewise use love as the highest value base. This is not as unrealistic as some may think at first blush. Indeed, it is eminently practical, but enough of that for now. The greatest good for the greatest number (a tip of my hat

to the Utilitarian thinkers from England) is actually an extension of loving our neighbors as we love ourselves. Freedom must be grounded in reciprocity.[16]

6. Free people and free nations must also be in general agreement on the definition of both personal and national "success". Success is becoming all that you can be in the economy of God's provision. Secularists and believers can agree on that general premise even though we have different ideas of how that takes place. What we do agree on, at a core level, is the obligation of society to attempt to provide a social climate where every citizen is not blocked by others' behavior from succeeding on the highest levels of their abilities, invested time, energy, and resources.

7. Free people and free nations need free access personally and socially to injections of spiritual truth and values. They need it as a kind of "social conscience", safeguarding society against the self-centeredness and abuse of power in fallen people and fallen institutions. Secularism is quarantining itself from spiritual truth at the great expense of the nations of the world. This current economic crisis is exhibit "A" of this phenomenon. Take spiritual truth out of the public square and you will have greed and exploitation quickly flooding in to fill the vacuum. Yet, this "sword" cuts both ways: create self-centered and socially irresponsible churches, that are not attempting to disciple their nations as Christ commanded, and are not equipping their people to do so, and you have exhibit "B" of the same problem. Uncontested secularism and irresponsible Christianity work together in destroying the possibility of free nations.

This book is not intended to be a primer on political science or even economics. It is merely pointing out the highlights of what moderately educated citizens should know about some of the basics of civil truths. Having read articles from the public newspapers of the eighteenth century in colonial America, I can assure you that the common citizen of that day was familiar with the issues I have raised. That being the

16. Matthew 10:8.

case, how "medicated" do you think the current citizens of your nation are? And what about the churches you are familiar with? How many of them are adequately educating their people on Kingdom truths that should be guiding and teaching the nations as they "observe all that I have commanded you"?[17]

I must now leave you with some very brutal facts all of us wish were not true. They address the magnitude of the real financial crisis here in the United States, which of course as the world's largest economy, affects everyone else. The European Union has its own set of ugly facts, as do Japan, China, and many other nations. All of us live in a measure of denial when confronted with the implications of these kinds of realities. May God grant us a clear sense of His control over where this may all lead and the courage to live in these facts, rather than try and run from them as many of our leaders are currently doing.

THE REAL NUMBERS OF OUR NATIONAL DEBT: THE CRISIS IS NOT A RECESSION

While doing economic research on labor unions in the 1960s, I had occasion to utilize the services of the U.S. Bureau of Labor Statistics; I came across multiple sets of other statistics on a number of other economic issues. As my trained economic theories were gradually murdered by ugly sets of practical realities in the real world, I came to truly appreciate Mark Twain's erudite comment, "There are lies, damn lies, and statistics."[18] Amen, brother. Statistics are often only as good as the people preparing them, for the purposes for which they were being prepared, by taking into account who was paying for them to be prepared and what they wanted those statistics to show.

I clearly understand why our national leaders, who actually know these facts, don't want them to be known for general consumption in society. They want to avoid a panic, impeachments, or the other possibilities of radical and unhelpful behavior. However, they are going to be known and leaders on every level of society need to know them sooner than later. Lives and property are at risk as well the viability of nations.

---

17. Matthew 28:20, NKJV.
18. Mark Twain, "Chapters from My Autobiography," North American Review, 1906-1907.

OUR REAL NATIONAL AND CUMULATIVE UNFUNDED
LIABILITIES TOTAL OVER $100 TRILLION

I cannot fathom how much money 100 trillion-plus dollars really is. I know about economic figures but however much we intellectually comprehend about figures like this, they are still almost unfathomable. This is especially true because this indebtedness is allegedly to be paid back by the after-tax revenues of the American people. I also know that it will not happen that way because monetary "games" will be played and a host of other negotiated tricks will be contrived. Regardless of all of this—the size of the nation's indebtedness, the business world's indebtedness, and the public's personal indebtedness—we have a mountain of debt large enough to crash the whole system and set us all back multiple generations in terms of the lifestyles that people in the Western world have come to believe they are "entitled" to.

Here is the most concise presentation of these figures I have seen. I trust their general reliability and have seen other figures like them and many estimates that are much larger. However, before we look at this, let us first remember that the $15 trillion figure currently being used does not include our estimated state debts of $2.8 trillion, which increases the total national debt to nearly $18 trillion. I want to further remind us that we are now entering the realm of discussing unfunded liabilities, where government agencies have indebtedness to pension funds, medical insurance funds, and the like which are legally binding but for which our governmental entities have no reserves accrued for these expenses. Here goes:

> "...U.S. states will run out of pension-fund money by 2025...aren't going to be able to make up those pension short-falls out of general tax revenue...So how much would the states have to book to fully fund those liabilities? Drop in another $3 Trillion...that takes us up to $19.5 Trillion (2011) in (state) liabilities. When you add in liabilities under Social Security and Medicare, in other words, when you account for the present value of those future payments in the same way that businesses have to account for the obligations they incur...a combined $106 Trillion in liabilities for Social Security and Medicare or

more than five times the total liabilities federal, state, and local debt we've totaled up so far...that's about twice the total private net worth of the United States.

"There is more, of course. Much more. Besides those monthly pension checks, the states are on the hook for retirees health care and other benefits to the tune of another one Trillion. And depending on how you account for it, another half Trillion or so...in liabilities related to the government guarantee of Fannie Mae and Freddie Mac and securities supported by the bailouts. Now, these aren't perfect numbers, but that's the rough picture: call it $130 Trillion or so, or just under ten times the official national debt."

Kevin D. Williamson, "The Other National Debt,"
The National Review, June 15, 2010, pp. 29-30

A QUICK LOOK AT OUR LIMITED OPTIONS

We do have a number of options for dealing with this debt, but none of them are good and all of them have massive negative potential implications:

1. We can offer to pay out our debts and obligations over longer periods of time and negotiate over the principal and interest amounts to be paid. However, try and calculate the interest payments alone on amounts of this magnitude or the years into the future it would take to pay them down in what can only be assumed to be massively inflated dollars. If you mathematically succeed, the amounts could send you to a mental institution.

2. We can sell off large amounts of government properties, offer to trade assets in lieu of money and therefore barter for asset exchanges or services of some kind. Once again, the owed amounts are so great that this seems highly unlikely.

3. We can default on the loans and bonds, or offer "take it or leave it" payment plans. Right. Who is going to buy our financial instruments ever again?

4. We can default on our obligations by inflating our money supply and thus pay back cents on the dollar, while at the same time totally destroying the net worth of all people living on fixed incomes or depending on retirements based on the value of current dollars.

5. We can do all of the above plus balance all government budgets on every level. Will that be enough? I have no idea, and I have yet to hear of anyone else who has one that is even remotely credible.

Welcome to our current situation. God is in it but to even call it a "great financial reset" is the kindest of terms. What an opportunity for our Daniels, Josephs, Deborahs, and assorted Churchills to come forth. How many of you reading this are saying, "This cannot be true, there must be some mistake." You are correct. There has been a series of very large mistakes. Yet, this is not the end of the world. It is likely to be the end of the ways we have managed the financial and social systems of the world as we have known them. Major changes will come and God's Kingdom will go forth and continue to yeast in the nations.

Let us move on now to our next chapter as we examine the nature of economics and some of the effects of centralization. Let us also agree to seek God for the courage to get off the "medications" being served us; we will all need clear heads to move through what is coming and to be fully available to God and others without being harassed by fear.

CHAPTER 4

ECONOMICS, CENTRALIZATION, AND THE QUESTION OF LIFESTYLE

"Experience should teach us to be most on our guard to protect liberty when the government's purposes are beneficent. Menborn to freedom are naturally alert to repel invasion of their liberty by evil-minded rulers. The greater dangers to liberty lurk in insidious encroachment by men of zeal, well-meaning but without understanding."

U.S. Supreme Court Justice Louis Brandeis,
Olmstead, et al. v. United States, 277 U.S. 438 (1928)

As we have seen, we are in a massive economic crisis, only partially revealed to most of our citizens, caused by citizens' irresponsible expectations of their governments, which were only too willing to accept those expectations that increased governments' power while resulting in the gradual forfeiting of their freedoms as citizens. All of this process was taking place in the context of an increasingly aggressive secularism and an increasingly numbed citizenry, indwelt by a slumbering church which had lost its mandate to disciple nations and seek first God's Kingdom. That is my general summary of where we have been so far.

Although this book is not a primer on either political theory or economics it unavoidably must deal with many of the most basic concepts of both.

The main focus of this book is to describe the realities of this economic and values crisis, and to point to where and how God's people might be of the utmost service to God and the people of the earth in the midst of it. However, until God's people see their responsibility to add to their evangelization of people on a personal level, the equally compelling mandate to disciple nations and address man's most fundamental social needs, neither our repentance for our omissions in this regard, nor our strategic operations to rectify it will be forthcoming. Therefore, God is going to use the pressures of this crisis to reorient His people and direct both them and their nations to the reality that His Kingdom truths have essential answers for our common dilemma.

THE EMERGENCE OF NEW LEADERS IN THIS CRISIS

I have implied since the outset of this book that this crisis is going to allow for the emergence of new leaders on every level of society and in every jurisdiction and nation, and remove large numbers of other ones. Problems promote us or hinder us according to our ability to deal with them. So it is with leadership: new leaders always emerge by the solving of problems the last set of leaders either helped create or couldn't navigate through once they saw them. I am personally expecting some highly gifted leaders to emerge from this crisis since it contains so many challenges on so many levels.

As we unwrap the challenges we face and some of my proposed answers to them here in this book, it should be clear to the reader that the solutions to these problems will be birthed in deep controversy and clothed in measures of personal sacrifice that few people will initially accept. The emerging leaders will be the ones who propose these answers on national or international levels—the leaders of governments and organizations that respond to them, and the leaders on local levels who help people walk through their often painful or disorienting outworkings. We are going to see many current social and economic paradigms cast off and numbers of new ones proposed. Some of them will be painful, and therefore offered reluctantly and received in the same way. The new leaders will be the ones birthing and nurturing this process on every level of society.

The "statesmen" and "stateswomen" by definition are leaders who are willing to lead people where they need to go for their own good and not necessarily the good of the leaders. They must be leaders who fear God and their own personal shortcomings, rather than the people they lead, save the damaging of them. Politicians may represent the people who elected them; statesmen and stateswomen take people to levels of achievement they could not attain without them. We will speak more about new leaders as we go.

GENERAL PRINCIPLES OF ECONOMICS
AND THE RESOLUTION OF THIS CRISIS

As many of you know, the word "economics" comes from the Greek word *oikos* (pronounced OY-kos), which literally means, the management of a household. It was assumed in man's earlier history that whatever responsible financial functions a civil form of government undertook for its citizens, those actions would be generally based on the way people responsibly cared for their own private households' financial matters. *Oikos* has obviously changed significantly, as modern economics emerged as a function of the modern state and the complexities of the modern marketplace. Many things brought about these changes but we will only deal with some of them.

In a very general sense, economics is about the management of man's labor and the management of the fruits of that labor, and its exchanges between others in the context of the values of the society in which these activities take place. Restating this from a biblical perspective, economics is about the organization of man's attempt to take dominion over the earth and the goals and practices governing it.[1] Economics is about choices, values, resources, and the rules and efficiencies measuring the process. As all of us know who are involved in trying to describe and manage the concepts and their applications, economics is at the same time both basically simple and highly complex.

Economic principles keep you and me alive, so to speak. They manage the systems that supply us with the material necessities of life and give

---

1. Genesis 1:26-28.

us a measure of blessings and the wonderful gift of having discretionary time, wherein we are not always working to simply stay alive. We live in a world of intelligent design built on the principles behind that design. The world of economics is no exception. It has laws and principles that govern what economic systems can produce and they are designed to operate at maximum efficiency so as to bless all who align themselves with those principles. Like every other discipline, economics also carries with it the penalties for breaking these principles. Wise economic policy is about seeking to discover these principles and apply them;[2] foolish economic policy is about trying to operate as if we can make up our own principles and force them upon the world.

Ultimately, economics is about aligning all these values, principles, and goals with God's view of them. When we do, we experience God's love for us, our love for Him, and the joys of seeing one another prosper according to God's will. The next chapters shall focus on four major economic principles I believe are most critical to understand at this time. They are: 1) the power of human choice in the marketplace, 2) the economic power of generational momentum, 3) the power of capital creation and employment incentives, and 4) the need for appropriate limits to financial leverage and currencies. In the process of addressing these core economic principles we will discuss them and their applications.

SUSTAINABLE ECONOMIC PROSPERITY
FOR THE GREATEST NUMBER OF PEOPLE

I have defined my economic goal for the nations as being that of seeing our world produce sustainable economic prosperity for the greatest number of people. I believe that is wholly consistent with the greatest commandment of loving God and loving our neighbor as ourselves. While "prosperity" is a relative word meaning different things to different people, if our individual goals for material and financial prosperity are rooted in God's will for us, and His service through us to others, prosperity will be contextualized properly.[3] What we do know

---

2. Proverbs 10:4; Matthew 25:14-30.
3. Proverbs 13:7-8; 14:24.

for sure is that God loves people and wants them to prosper in Him and be free from abuse and exploitation, even though He may temporarily use those devices to hone our character or redirect our paths.

"Sustainability" deals with issues like long-term strategic thinking and planning regarding competitive advantages, long-term market share and resource availability, effects on the environment and related social issues, and the future effects on coming generations of our current values and actions. Short-term thinking is all about greed, quick returns on investments and the minimization of labor or capital, and single generation consumption based on personal advantages. We are in this current crisis because of the abuses of short-term and self-centered thinking driving our economic policies.

"Prosperity" should easily be understood to mean the ability to supply a standard of living for all people that reflects the value of their contributions into the economy, gives the general population a lifestyle free of fear for basic human needs, and offers an attainable possibility of upward economic mobility within a just economic system for those who want to earn it. It also must provide the ability to educate and care for the needs of those genuinely requiring social assistance.

In terms of "the greatest number of people", any system that only allows or encourages the multi-talented or "insiders" to prosper, and leaves out everyone else, reflects a disdain for all others created in God's image and not a love and respect for humanity. Anyone who truly understands and values the concept of community lives in the reality that love leaves no one behind and does not forget those in need, even if they have brought this condition upon themselves. Community demands that as the apostle Paul says, "And if one member suffers, all the members suffer with it; and if one member is honored, all the members rejoice with it."[4] National community is built one local community at a time. A healthy church will help create transformed local communities as a part of the threefold cord of extending Christ's love. Healthy people rejoice in the prosperity of all who have earned or experienced it by God's hand.

---

4. 1 Corinthians 12:26.

QUESTIONS THAT ECONOMICS AND OUR WORLDVIEW
BRING TO THE MANAGEMENT OF NATIONS

Here is a general list of the kinds of questions and issues that economics forces us to deal with:

1. What economic inequalities are morally acceptable and why?

2. What kinds of business practices are unfair and why?

3. What consumption levels are socially destructive because they feed improper levels of consumerism, consumption, and debt that corrupt our character?

4. What is the difference between exploiting the earth's resources and harvesting them for the betterment of mankind?

5. What role, if any, should the government have in setting prices in any area?

6. Why did Jesus say, "the poor you have with you always,"[5] and what does that mean relative to our desire to reduce or eliminate poverty?

7. How do we grow businesses or national economies without producing consumer debt through emotion-driven advertising and financial manipulation?

8. How do we extend charity or aid programs without rewarding destructive behavior or indolence?

9. What wage and economic policies will most specifically strengthen families, especially families with small children needing parental care?

10. How should we regulate currencies so as to prevent inflation or unfair trade advantages?

11. What is the fairest and most just level of taxation policy that pays for appropriate social services but does not hinder the necessary growth of the economy?

---

5. Matthew 26:11.

12. Is using the cheaper labor from a foreign country fair to them, or one's own domestic labor forces, in order to produce domestic services or products here at home at cheaper prices?

13. When does the notion of a nation's essential businesses becoming "too big to fail" do harm to a nation's best economic interests?

14. What levels should be the maximum leverage rates for currencies within our banking systems, and who should establish oversight of banks?

15. What role should the government play in medical insurances and retirement programs?

16. What historically has created the highest private investment rates and maximized employment rates in the nations of the world?

17. When should the government give preferential treatment to any class of people for employment or financial advantages?

The questions could go on and on. We can all see that economic issues are almost everywhere and therefore, as citizens of both God's Kingdom and of our nations, we need principled answers to guide our lives and national policies. As virtually all educated people know, economic issues are repeatedly at or near the top of all national issues in public elections. The reason for that is simple: economics defines employment rates and educational and lifestyle issues for citizens and touches virtually all areas of their material wants and needs. God is fully aware of that and Jesus addressed lifestyle issues. The Old Testament is full of economic observations, especially in the book of Proverbs. Economic issues define the power of nations and reflect the worldview and values of their systems.

Until the church takes up its responsibility to teach what the Scriptures say about economic issues, we should not expect the general public to have sufficient economic knowledge to elect public officials capable of helping nations attain sustainable prosperity for the greatest number of people. It really is that simple. How important is this? What does this current crisis tell us?

ECONOMIC GOALS FOR DISCIPLING NATIONS

> "The idea that the gospel is addressed only to the individual and that it is only indirectly addressed to societies, nations, and cultures is simply an illusion of our individualistic post-Enlightenment Western culture. Very plainly when we turn to the Old Testament we find no such separation of the individual from the society which nurtures and forms him and of which he is a part."
>
> Lesslie Newbigin, *The Gospel in a Pluralist Society,* 1989, p. 199

It is no small challenge to put together a priority list of the most compelling components of a Kingdom-based economic system or "wish list", for two reasons: 1. Will it be accurate and axiomatically based (contain truly seminal principles) rather than a set of secondary economic results or functions? and 2. How "realistic" can the list be when we know many of our goals are not currently possible in this secularly constructed economic order? Nevertheless, here is a set of preliminary concepts and goals to at least start a serious discussion with those who see the need to do so. I also note that while many of the items in this list specifically address economic issues here in the United States, I believe they would be principally useful for all nations as points of policy discussions. These points have a clear relationship to biblical principles in the Scriptures.

1. A global network of Christian economists and theologians should be formed, who are willing to be part of a project to compile teaching materials for general distribution to churches, organizations, governments, etc., and be available for consulting on related issues. This group would be an active resource for all denominations, apostolic church networks, and interested groups and associations willing to participate. Members of this group would certainly not agree on all things (a room filled with three economists has at least five different opinions on economic issues), but they would stimulate and produce important information for the task of discipling nations and their social structures. This group is doing the work of analyzing and seeking to apply spiritual principles to national social systems within the threefold cord of discipling nations.

2. We need a balanced recognition of the need for individual achieve-
    ment within the economic system, combined with the need for a
    community ethic that cares for those who are in genuine need of
    care, or provides the training and the opportunity to become self-
    sufficient and productive. Those elements of the so-called "left"
    and "right" (individual rights and a functioning sense of commu-
    nity), need to merge.

3. We need an economy that strongly supports the formation and
    enhancement of nuclear family structures as the primary so-
    cialization-training group within the society.[6] As we will see in
    chapter 6, the economic momentum of families across the gen-
    erations is a critical element in God's plan to bless the nations.

4. We need a grossly simplified federal taxation system that taxes
    all citizens and businesses at the same base rate (20 percent
    maximum, based on the Old Testament's tithe levels).[7] We will
    discuss this subject and some of the modifications arising from it
    in chapter 7.

5. All social safety net programs would also be administrated on a
    local level, evaluating people's genuine needs based on a rela-
    tional knowledge of them. This mirrors the way the poor tithe
    was administered locally in Israel. Centralized government char-
    ity or safety net compensations currently take place on an imper-
    sonal and non-relationally based level of ignorance.

6. We need balanced civil budgets on all levels of government,
    with carefully crafted language so as to eliminate attempts to
    circumvent the laws.

7. We need asset-backed currencies. Realistically, this would have to
    take place as a gradual process which would begin at rates steep
    enough to change the system but not so steep as to shut it down.
    This policy would have major stabilizing effects on inflation, banking,
    and the solidification of the entire system as it adjusts to it.

---

6. Genesis 12:3.
7. Deuteronomy 14:28-29.

8. We need to restructure the current banking system in the United States and make the central banking system fully controlled by an extension of both the states and the federal government.

9. We need a broader and more comprehensive national strategic plan which establishes and implements the core requirements for our reserves in terms of food, water, energy, strategic metals, national industries, and whatever else secures the nation from potential material shortages, national disasters, or wars.

10. We need to require that only national citizens, or those with resident status, receive the benefits of our social services on a regular basis. This obviously will require resolution of our immigration problems here in the United States.

11. We need to redirect charity and economic training programs as much as is possible back to the private sector. Programs that are not relationally based, but rather institutionally-based, are notorious for their ineffectiveness and bureaucratic misuse of funds. Much could be said about this.

12. We need a reorganization as soon as possible of all levels of government structures and programs to eliminate redundancies that are costing multiple billions of dollars annually in misspent time, money, bureaucratic inefficiencies, and needless inter-agency competition.

This is just a short list of places to begin our discussions. Since God does not honor poor stewardship, small wonder our civil governments are broke, even beyond their unbiblical jurisdictional financial misappropriations.

CENTRALIZATION: SOME CHALLENGES AND BENEFITS

"In fifty years, a historian will look back at the protests of 2011 and describe the global crisis as a symptom of the end of a uniquely 20th century phenomenon: the state took unprecedented control of individuals' lives, and its role grew out of proportion until it finally cracked."

Nadim Shehadi, "The Burden of a Long Century,"
New York Times – Today, January 15, 2012, p. 2

Historian Paul Johnson, in his bestseller *Modern Times,* powerfully and clearly pointed out that the twentieth century saw the greatest centralizing of power among civil governments in man's history.[8] Modernity is characterized by this centralization and now, in the twenty-first century, civil government's inability to pay for the reality of that process is upon the nations.

Centralizing power, or solidifying organizations by creating significant mass in terms of skilled people and financial resources, is not necessarily wrong or even unbiblical so long as it is not at the expense of the other jurisdictions of government. In fact, in cases like the defense of a nation and the creation of its military resources, it is essential. The problem with centralization is its tendencies to create inefficient bureaucracies, duplications of work and organizational structures, weakening in a society's other government structures, and the lessening of personal responsibility within other areas of the culture or nation. The centralization of civil governments in Western nations has done all of these negative things. Most glaringly, the process is bankrupting these governments.

Another challenging result of these massive civil governments is the consolidation of lobbying activities surrounding them from the private sector. This is especially true for large corporations and the undue influence that the effects of this lobbying has had on nations' policy directions. This has also created the formation of a governing elite of "revolving doors" so to speak, between elected officials and corporate leaders who go in and out of government positions of power and thus create what James Madison referred to as "factions". Madison, a Founding Father, vigorously warned us of their potential threats to democracy in his famous essay in *The Federalist Papers.*[9]

---

8. Paul Johnson, Modern Times (New York: HarperPerennial, 1992).
9. James Madison, "The Same Subject Continued, [Essay] No. 10," in The Federalist Papers, New American Library ed. (New York: New American Library, 1961), 77-84.

THE POTENTIAL CHALLENGE OF STATE CAPITALISM

As these alliances between government leaders and departments, corporations, non-governmental organizations (NGOs), and the academic elite continue to solidify, growing numbers of social commentators are referring to the emergence of "State Capitalism" and its gradual possibilities of morphing into fascism. Obviously, communism and fascism are twin forms of authoritarian civil government differing primarily in how they relate to economic planning, in a macro sense, in their respective economies. In the one, the state does the planning and execution, and in the other, the state and corporate world plan together and work out the execution of their plans within their respective spheres of operation. Both forms of this governmental centralization diminish the rights of citizens as more and more of the citizens' decisions are either directly or indirectly made for them by civil leaders, the courts, and the economic planners, be they governmental decision makers or corporate leaders.

This financial crisis has the potential to seriously alter this unhealthy alliance between large corporate powers and civil government. Once again I call the reader's attention to the fact that "capitalism" is not, by definition, the culprit here. Rather, it is the inadequate hindrances to these alliances, which takes the process of decision-making—greatly affecting the public welfare—outside of the public's input, further strengthening the power of monopoly being exercised by these corporate giants.

Virtually all of us are familiar with Lord Acton's dictum, "Power tends to corrupt and absolute power corrupts absolutely."[10] To the degree that this is true, it is true because of man's fallen nature. As already discussed, this is the reason the United States' civil government has sought inherent remedy from this abuse of power through the separation of powers and its three branches of government (executive, legislative, and judicial); in addition, the Scriptures teach the multi-jurisdictions of government already cited. Nevertheless, the centralization of civil government over the last century has sidestepped these guardrails and

---

10. Lord John Acton, *Letter to Bishop Mandell Creighton*, April 5, 1887.

created both the threat to liberty and the financial crisis we are entering now. I am personally convinced that this crisis is going to be used by God to not only severely alter this centralization, but to maintain decentralization for as long as His people have the clarity of Kingdom truth to maintain it. This is one of the core premises of this study.

All of these issues are related to the discussions of federalism, states' rights, and the nature and interpretation of our U.S. Constitution. These same questions of governmental structure are relevant in all nations of the world. As this crisis unfolds and intensifies, the public is going to be forced to deal with these issues and theories of political philosophy, and continue to both pay for our ignorance that got us here as well as make critical political choices to resolve them. Christians must be at the center of these discussions on both local and national levels. This means that the church leaders who would disciple nations, must begin to do so first in their own pulpits. The day is coming when the Holy Spirit is going to remove any church leaders' "excuses" for committing this sin of not educating their people and serving their fellow man by giving them truth, because the sounds crying out for it to be done will have been so loud in the streets of their nations.

PRINCIPLES OF KINGDOM STRUCTURES—INSIDE-OUT VS. OUTSIDE-IN AND BOTTOM-UP VS. TOP-DOWN: CREATING AND CONNECTING UNITS OF INTEGRITY

This section's heading is long indeed and could well be the makings of a short book itself. We will deal with these issues as we go on but they also must be noted here while we are addressing centralization and related issues. Let's begin with building from the inside-out versus building from the outside-in.

The secular philosophies of centralization view changing the social attitudes and structures of their citizens as best achieved by creating and passing endless series of laws designed to regulate behavior by applying external legal force. Laws and regulations are external forms of force. Christ and His Kingdom are built on the principle of changing citizens' hearts and internal attitudes and thinking mechanisms rather than attempting to change them from the "outside-in."[11] Christians are "born again to see the Kingdom," because it requires inner-sight to change the inner-self.[12] God changes His people by changing their hearts and then their heads. The secular world attempts to do so by social conditioning; the King does it by spiritually transferring His values and point of view into His subjects supernaturally—from an entirely different method than outside external social conditioning. As we will soon see in our next chapter, on "The Power of Human Choice and Economics," internal human choice is infinitely more powerful than applying external pressures to modify man's choices or behavior.

The top-down versus bottom-up distinction is of a similar nature. The world system generally believes, by evidence of its behavior, that people are changed by leaders pressing upon them the leaders' decisions or opinions. The Kingdom of God holds that free men and free women are free because of the truths they hold within themselves, having come to those decisions by working them through internally in a process with God.[13] Leaders can and should lead by example and surely can inspire and give insight and information for their followers to process and work through. Yet, the core national strength of any people or nation is measured by the degree to which their hearts are internally united by having come to similar conclusions through their own internal processes.

Relative to the truth that healthy large organizations are only created by adding together healthy smaller units, this truth should be obvious to anyone who has built anything from a model car, to a house or organization of any kind. However, it seems to be not that obvious to many government organizations. They insist that their operations be built from the top-down and the outside-in, in spite of their multiple redundancies and inefficiencies. They believe they can and will create "strength" for all the other lesser agencies which report to them. If their thinking is actually related to the real world of truth, all structurally sound buildings should begin construction on the top floor and

11. Jeremiah 31:31-34; Ezekiel 36:26-27.
12. John 3:3, 5.
13. John 8:32.

work their way down to the foundations. The examples and absurdities of this kind of thinking are legendary among those working with organizations that think this way. They also waste enormous amounts of human energy and money.

All of these principles will weave themselves into our following discussions regarding economic issues and principles. Suffice to say, one has to wonder why some ideas which have so thoroughly disproven themselves repeatedly still parade on as if reality is the imposter and not them.

QUESTIONS OF LIFESTYLE IN THE MODERN WORLD

We have to ask the question, for integrity's sake, what level of lifestyle is appropriate for the citizens of a healthy nation? I am not presuming that one lifestyle should fit all in a healthy nation, but rather, from an economic perspective, should economically-driven consumption rates force its citizens to consume goods and services at rates that they otherwise would not choose in a healthy society? This question is not so much a "capitalism" question as much as it is what kind of capitalism are we going to choose to drive our values and lifestyles? The current system, driven by the forced consumption rates required to service both personal and government debt, owes its core thanks to John Maynard Keynes, the modern architect of the world's global economic system. Tempted though I may be to follow through on a discussion of Mr. Keynes, suffice to say, man should have an economic system that serves him rather than a system he must serve.

Currently that question must be put on the table. Economic systems are "neutral". They are designed to create economic conditions and results that conform to the values, which drive them. They are not impersonal machines; they are systems that reflect the worldview and values of the people designing and utilizing them. In today's modern economies we increasingly have planned obsolescence; the inability to find products that can be repaired but instead must be discarded; the disappearance of whole crafts and industries; the swallowing up of small businesses locally by major corporations going national or global, etc., etc., etc.

I am neither a Luddite nor anti-market systems: I am simply saying that this values and debt crisis offers us all opportunities to discuss these issues on an unprecedented level and we must not miss it. This discussion must be led by the Christians, if we are capable of so doing. If it is led by political parties or sub-pressure groups it will be woefully inadequate and driven by political agendas. Once again, I am raising a very critical issue that is part of the multi-dimensional set of issues this economic crisis is creating. May God help His people to see what this means for us as an opportunity to serve God by serving His nations.

So let us now go straight into the economic discussions for which we have attempted to prepare with these opening four chapters. There is so much to say but our initial capacities for deeper discussions, for most believers, will not yet allow them. Even for many of us as leaders these topics have lain outside of our past concerns or responsibilities, as we perceived them. Now God is moving them front and center.

CHAPTER 5

ON THE POWER OF HUMAN
CHOICE AND ECONOMICS

Love is the most powerful force on earth. Human love is driven by the power of choice. Choice commits to love someone or something and then endures, as the apostle Paul says, whatever obstacles that would seek to remove it. So it is with economics; personal human choice drives the marketplace more powerfully than any other force. The power of "choice" is the real energy behind the "invisible hand" that Adam Smith was pointing toward in his attempt to explain the dynamic that drives the marketplace and makes it perform as it does.[1]

Not all human choices benefit others. Therefore, we need to regulate and even prohibit some of them. Trust in the system is produced when regulation and values combine to keep the system honest and ethical. The question then becomes: Who is to do that regulation, the state, the private sector, or both? Now we are into one of the great questions of the day. If our answer to this question practically works and keeps the marketplace growing and fair, then the citizens using the marketplace will have faith in their economic system. Faith in the system, after the power of choice and trust, is the next great dynamic of the marketplace. Limit choices unwisely, or fail to regulate or prohibit what is required, and the loss of faith will bring the system into a stall

---

1. Adam Smith, *The Theory of Moral Sentiments* (London: A. Millar, 1759).

or worse. So there we have the "trinity" of a dynamic marketplace: choice, trust, and faith. While other important dynamics exist, these are the glue that holds them all in place under God's watchful eye.

In this chapter, then, we shall be dealing with a number of important issues all related in some way to these three major dynamics of the marketplace. They all begin in some direct way with the issue of choices and the consequences which those choices create. Moses reminds us that the issues of life and death, and thereby the issues of prosperity or failure are both linked to the power to choose given to us by a loving Father:

> "I call heaven and earth to witness against you today,
> that I have set before you life and death, the blessing and
> the curse. So choose life in order that you may live."
>
> Deuteronomy 30:19

Christ offers choice to mankind in the New Testament as well. It really is all about "whosoever will may come." In the mysterious intertwining of the sovereignty of God and the will of man, all of humanity works out their lives on a daily basis of multiple choices, all of which combine to form a character and ultimately a life story. The mandate of loving our neighbor therefore ought to be lived out in a society whose social systems seek to maximize choice by fostering behavior free of force, manipulation, or improper dependency on others. Love honors others' choices and attempts to only interrupt the process of choice when its consequences will bring harm, injustice, or the loss of freedom to others.[2] This then should be the ideal that we seek to inject into the marketplace and all other dimensions of human culture and relationships.

God honors all human activity that aligns itself with His principles of life and the aims for His Kingdom.[3] This means that being a Christian, relative to the effects of our actions or the dynamics of our social systems, is only of relative value. In this sense the issue becomes: Do some individuals' actions or their nation's actions align themselves with the general principles of the Kingdom or not? If they do, they will produce a measure of good results whether the ones taking those

---

2.   1 Corinthians 13.
3.   Isaiah 48:17-19.

actions are believers or not. For example, because God honors the act of investing in the sound character of our children,[4] Christian or not, God will honor that activity as much as He deems possible relative to His plan for those people who are practicing this admirable action. Large numbers of "saved" Christians practice economic principles aligned with the world system's economic values and not the Kingdom's. The fruit of their economic choices therefore will be as a result of their errant choices rather than their admirable faith in Christ.

Economically speaking, because financial savings and strategic spending are biblical values, a nation's savings rates give an indication of the values within that nation and hence the ability to trust in its economic health, all other things being equal as we say in economic discussions. Its alignment with Kingdom values in this regard gives it an economic advantage regardless of how many unsaved people that nation may contain. This reality of Kingdom values alignment, or misalignment, will show up in our discussions again and again. Our goal, economically or politically speaking, is not to get everyone "saved" but rather to get everyone, saved or unsaved, aligning their lifestyles and social systems with Kingdom values. That alignment will maximize both the citizens' freedom and their possibility of seeing that obedience to those values actually works in the real world, and hence there may indeed be somebody behind those values (God). I call this "evangelism through results" or "Kingdom net fishing". We will also discuss this in greater detail in a later chapter. Let us move on now to another point of introduction before we turn to unwrapping the issues surrounding human labor and its relationship to the economic health of a nation.

> "But you shall remember the LORD your God, for it is He
> who is giving you power to make wealth, that He may confirm
> His covenant which He swore to your fathers, as it is this day."
> Deuteronomy 8:18

The four major economic principles on which we are focusing in this book, beyond the challenges of centralization, are the ones I believe most prominently relate to the power to create wealth. They are:

---

4. Deuteronomy 6:4-9.

1. The power of choice.

2. The power of generational momentum.

3. The linkage of capital creation with incentives for employment training and job creation.

4. The necessity of appropriate financial limits and the need for asset-backed currencies.

All of these principles are core principles and essential to the foundation of a sound economy aligned with God's Kingdom social values. While there are a myriad of other economic issues, such as trade policies, subsidies, competitive advantages, etc., etc., etc., these four axiomatic economic issues touch most specifically on the ability to walk out the blessings of wealth creation offered to us by Moses in the above quote. The covenant of God is one of mutual responsibility.[5] Man takes responsibility to learn to practice God's values and principles in the context of his relationship to God and his neighbor, and God in turn takes responsibility to protect His people from obstacles to their relationship with Him. The power to create wealth is the power to obey God, but that power is only released by knowing specifically what principles specifically apply in any particular activity. Obviously, I have written this book in an attempt to address these principles so as to both enhance our relationship with God, and challenge us to become well versed enough in the application of these truths to bring them to the nations in which we live. In so doing we can offer them to God as an act of obedience and love, and see the blessing of God upon the nations practicing them. Christ died for the nations and loves them. When love is linked to obedience, it releases God's joy and our prosperity of soul and circumstances.

THE NATURE OF LABOR AND ITS RELATIONSHIP TO A JUST AND PROSPEROUS ECONOMY

The foundation of all economic activity is labor. Labor creates something to be sold or traded and thus compensated. Every other economic activity

---

5. Deuteronomy 28:1-2, 15; John 1:12.

is related to this most basic starting point. Yet, that labor first originated in the process of thought. A vision or motivation to create something or take some action first begins internally before it makes its way out into the material world. Economic activity then truly begins on the internal level. We are now ready to discuss the process of incarnation.

THE BEAUTY OF LABOR AND THE GIFT OF INCARNATION

Ideas have limited value until they are lived out or incarnated. Incarnation is generally understood to be the process of something moving from the realm of the abstract or ethereal into the realm of the concrete.[6] Ideas or visions need to be incarnated to become of practical use. Labor is the process whereby incarnation takes place. Physical energy is expended to facilitate this process of incarnation. Ideas without delivery systems remain simply ideas.

Labor that is done unto God and for God's pleasure is a form of worship. Therefore, since God loves people and has commanded us to love them as well, labor that is genuinely blessing people and adding to their value, is also a form of worship. Indeed, God has established labor specifically designed for each and every one of His children to perform. This Scripture tells us exactly that:

"For we are His workmanship, created in Christ Jesus for good works, which God prepared beforehand that we would walk in them."
Ephesians 2:10

This is a magnificent truth and one that should create a deep hunger in the hearts of all who perceive its meaning to diligently seek to discover exactly what work God has prepared them to enter into. God Himself ordained and modeled satisfying labor and the joy of incarnating ideas and visions into the material universe.[7]

GOD-ORDAINED LABOR IS A FORM OF WORSHIP

Hebrew experts remind us that the word *avodah* is commonly translated either "work" (labor) or "worship". Something that clearly shows how

---

6. John 1:14.
7. Genesis 2:1-3.

many Christians don't understand this is how commonly they speak of heaven and eternity being a place where work has vanished since it was "part of the curse." Few ideas have hurt us more than this one. Christians should be the most valuable workers on earth since their labor is rooted in God and energized by Him. Since labor is the foundation of economic activity, can you imagine an economy filled with God-ordained labor and what it would look like and produce for its people? That is what I expect to see in eternity.

The root of the word *avodah* means "to labor or serve". The cluster of words derived from this word gives us insight into the nature of labor and worship. An *oveid* is a worker. An *eved* is a slave. *Avudut* is slavery. Work, or labor, involves the idea of serving someone. *Avodut elohim* is the service or worship of the true God. *Avodah zarah* is literally "strange worship". *Avodat elilim* is idolatry, the worship of false gods. Indeed, false worship or idolatry is in essence serving the devil and leads to *avudut*—bondage, slavery, and to Satan himself. The insight into the language here comes from a man named William D. Bjoraker.[8]

Worship of the true God is not always easy. Worship is sometimes a rigorous discipline required of us when we are going through difficult or hard times in order to keep us aligned with the purposes God has given us to gain from those circumstances. Worship is not just singing around the campfire or in the sanctuary. The world cannot be transformed without labor that is aligned with God's purposes. That process must begin with many believers first experiencing a major change in the way they view their work and the spirit in which they practice it. Once we see a truth, guess what the next step is? We have the choice to apply it. We are back at the beginning now; to help change our economy, we Christians must choose to lead the way on the most basic level. We must choose to find the labor we are designed to do and do it unto the Lord. Secular economists and political parties have no idea what we are talking about here but I am sure you do. Now we must face up to it.

---

8.   William D. Bjoraker, "Word Study (Avodah) – Work/Worship," Assemblies of God.org. http://ag.org/top/church_workers/wrshp_gen_avodah.cfm.

MY LABOR SHOWS THE REAL ME: DISCOVERING OUR DIVINE LABOR

Labor is the process through which I reveal my internal reality to the external world. My labor reflects and reveals my character, disciplines, views of excellence, commitment to service, and my active grasp of my God-ordained gifts and passions. I have maintained for decades that "God pays for what He orders." This means there are divine reservoirs of energy and creativity waiting to be released into my labor through the gifts and life passions stirring in my redeemed heart. As I see and embrace what my Creator has put within me, my ministry and my worship fuse into what I now call my work or my labor.

In our search for our assigned form of labor there are a set of clues to follow. What are the patterns of our passions that were alive in us even before we may have known God? Frequently we engaged in parts of our calling, distorted as they may have been, even when we were in the world, so to speak. Ask the Holy Spirit and ask those you know and trust: "What skills or passions do you see in me that bring me to life when you see me exercising them?" "How do you see me adding value to people and bringing life out of them with my words or actions?" These kinds of questions will lead us to seeing things that will appear so obvious we will marvel that we did not see them sooner. Do you love to teach, serve, create with your hands? What hobbies have always given you joy or a special sense of excitement? What kind of work would you do if the world were yours? It is never too late to find your calling and invest in it. God is committed to helping us answer these questions and find ways to help us live out the answers. When we are in our assigned labor we can feel God's pleasure when we work. Those of you who are already there know exactly what I am saying. Your labor "fits you and you fit it."

AUTHORIZED LABOR AND SUCCESS

"I can do nothing on My own initiative. As I hear, I judge;
and My judgment is just, because I do not seek My own
will, but the will of Him who sent Me."

John 5:30

Another way of saying all of this is that the goal of every believer should be to engage daily in what we might call authorized labor. Authorized labor was the only kind of labor that Jesus would engage. Authorized labor is the work God has ordained for us to do from the heavenly realm, bringing it to the earthly realm. Entering God's assigned labor helps us learn how to "enter His rest", to cite the phrase used in Hebrews 4. There is peace in doing what we are called to do even though all labor here on earth has portions of it that stretch us and force discipline upon us.

How we define "success" will define how we see our mission. We must therefore be very clear on that definition, what it means to us, and whether we are losing sight of it in the midst of challenges to it. Simply stated, success is obeying God and letting the fruits of that obedience originate in Him. Jesus repeatedly modeled this for us and a re-reading of John 17 is always a great reminder of this truth. Success in God is not about money, fame, fortune, or accolades from crowds. Success is about seeking first the Kingdom of God, and loving Him and our neighbor as ourselves. Success is finding your gifts and assigned labor (ministry), and living them out with energy and gratitude. Touching on the money issue, the question is not how much money we may make; the issue is having enough money to fulfill our God-ordained mission and the lifestyle He has set for us, and sowing into His Kingdom work whatever He says to do. Prosperity, or the financial lack thereof, should only be relative to our calling. I remind us of Paul's admonition in Ephesians 4:28, "He who steals must steal no longer; but rather he must labor, performing with his own hands what is good, in order that he will have something to share with one who has need."

Ultimately, success is fulfilling our obedience to God and His service to others through us here on earth, and acquiring the skill sets and character He desires to carry with us into eternity. Life here on earth is in a real sense our training for eternity. Our so-called rewards in eternity will be largely based on building upon what we brought home to eternity from our journey here in the dimension of time. The skill sets of character will pass through the "fire" of death.[9] A more advanced dis-

---

9. 1 Corinthians 3:12-15.

cussion of this defining of success would entail the walking in sufficient spiritual maturity to pull eternity into a space-time world and bring the future power of Kingdom life into this world now. That is exactly what Jesus modeled for us. His complete obedience to the Father allowed Him to pull eternity into time.

CAPITALISM AND THE ISSUE OF ALIENATED LABOR

Alienated labor is labor that is not related to people's calling or labor that dehumanizes people by simply using them without concern for their dignity, needs, or inherent desire to find meaning in their labor. Capitalism, like all systems of employed labor, has been particularly susceptible to this accusation and practice. The socialist and Marxist critiques of capitalism have pounded away on this issue for decades, especially in academic circles. It is an entirely legitimate concern for any economy based on any other supreme ethic, such as profit, than the one we are using here in our discussion. One cannot love their neighbor as themselves and use his or her labor in an alienated fashion. Love does not exploit, it enhances. All of us familiar with this issue and holding a passion for social and economic justice could cite numerous examples, both historic and current, of this using of people by the capitalistic system. In my earlier days I considered myself as a "soft" Marxist while studying at the university. I could speak somewhat authoritatively on the subject of alienated labor and its effects on societies and people. On the other hand, few societies in history have used their citizens for "the sake of the vision" more than the modern Marxist societies. I say again, no system will seek to avoid alienated labor consistently unless it is constantly infused with a Christian ethic of love. That is not idealism; it is simple economic fact in a world driven by fallen people and systems driven by "the revolution", or the single-minded need for profit.

Many of us are weary of the "left-right" arguments, wherein both straw man arguments and real arguments fuel the passions of both sides. Capitalism wins the argument hands down on the issue of sheer productivity and the rapidity of growth of upward economic mobility. However, the abuse of power, especially on the levels of capitalism furthest away from their employees, suppliers, and customers, and the effects of their policies on them, are the prime offenders of both alienated labor and the dehumanizing of people connected with their activities. Lest we wring our hands too much and point our fingers at those doing so, while we are using their products and living off the benefits of the capitalistic lifestyle, we would all do well to ponder our own roles in this situation. There is more than enough culpability to go around. The point is to infuse the productive machine with people and values that minimize problems and keep in check the sectors of the economy most susceptible to abuses. For Christianity, the solution to this problem begins with addressing the dearth of teaching and equipping going on in our pulpits and small group meetings, and the challenging of our people to acquire a matured Christianity that lives unto God and disciples nations.

Until the Christian community, with multiple hundreds of millions of alleged believers, decides to both model within itself both sides of the "productivity-none left out" debates, and wisely and vigorously engages the social systems of the world, nothing positive can come out of the debate being generated by the current economic crisis. And yes, that is why I am writing this book.

THE ENGINE OF ECONOMIC CHOICE:
THE PRIVATE SECTOR, THE GOVERNMENT,
AND THE EMERGENCE OF THE BUREAUCRATIC ELITE

Capitalism is not going away and neither is the civil government and its role in the economy. The challenge therefore is to find our way into injecting into nations' value systems the values, principles, and practices that will most align themselves with God's Kingdom. These injections must operate in the context of secular societies or even societies wherein their religious orientations are hostile to Judeo-Christian ethics in political-economic arenas. Let us first address the overall tensions between the so-called free market capitalist and the mixed economy advocates.

CHALLENGES OF REGULATION AND FREE MARKET EFFICIENCIES

This discussion is historically long, intense, and often very complicated when it drops down into specific cases and proposed applications.

What is clear to virtually all of us who deal with these questions is that the argument realistically is not should the civil government intervene in the marketplace, but rather when and how much. In a fallen world, particularly in a world where Christian values are not sought out or seen as relevant to economic issues, regulation is required to keep in check the effects of greed, unwarranted speculations by those holding public funds (retirement pension funds, for example) and the like. Exhibit "A" of the need for regulation is the current catastrophe brought about by the financial community in the private sector, the public servants in federal housing programs (Freddie Mac and Fannie Mae), and the almost total lack of financial responsibility exhibited by the banking system dealing with home loans and mortgages. This fiasco will shut down the proponents of "free market" economics for a long, long, time. A mixed economy will always exist in a fallen world of sin. As already noted, the Scriptures place the responsibility on civil government for national defense and the economic issues that surround a nation's ability to sustain its social systems in the face of disaster or war.

Having said that, my own stand is very simple and based on biblical principles: all economic policies should maximize private choice and freedoms as they promote ethical self-government, and utilize civil intervention only where the private sector is proving itself unable to regulate justice and a level playing field for all citizens. The more we lean on the civil government for regulation the less personally responsible the citizens become for their own lives. Creating dependency in others is not about loving them unless their inability to care for themselves is permanent and required. Unwarranted dependency is a subtle form of slavery being practiced in the name of "aid".

> "The doctrine of unintended consequences turns the eyes of the political economist away from the moral intentions of individuals and toward the final social consequences of their actions. More than that, it turns his attention to systems *qua* systems."
>
> Michael Novak, *The Spirit of Democratic Capitalism*, 1991, p. 89

The other dimension of this question regarding government interventions tends to deal with the civil government's attempt to correct market variables such as unemployment, inflation, "desired" support for particular industries or markets, and other variables the civil "experts" feel they, rather than inherent market mechanisms, will correct. This is where the greatest heat between the various positions is generated. The economic term "unintended consequences" was created to explain the sometimes huge differences between what a particular government program was supposed to create and what it actually did create. Some of these unintended consequences are legendary, and I am sure that the federal housing program's loan policies which helped create the current foreclosure of millions of American home loans will make the long list. Nevertheless, civil government is required to oversee trade laws and a host of other issues dealing with international economic events.

Economists are famous for the language of uncertainties; you will seldom ever hear a policy statement not ending in the caveats "other things remaining equal," or "in the long run." Since global markets are made up of multiple millions of decisions being made daily by billions of people, all things remaining equal is not likely to happen. There certainly are trends, long run trends, and economic principles that govern and modify results of decisions. As all of you engaged in these things know, these issues form the dividing lines between the Keynesians and the Austrian School economists. F. A. Hayek, one of the fathers of the Austrian School has made an interesting and relevant comment regarding all of this: "If one tries to create a truly planned society, one will not be able to separate our control of the economy from political control."[10] A more liberal response would point out the need for essential government services. The real argument should go back to what we discussed in chapter 3; that is, based on the biblical notion of governmental jurisdictions and jurisdictional problem-solving, which of the five jurisdictions should be involved in these financial issues, and why and how much is required to pay for these services? What is undeniably clear today is that civil government

10. Friedrich A. Hayek, *The Road to Serfdom: Text and Documents*, rev. ed., ed. Bruce Caldwell (1944; Chicago: University of Chicago Press, 2007). Citation refers to 2007 edition.

has engaged in services it cannot pay for and the money required to get us out of this problem will be hard pressed to come through the route of taxation without further shutting down the global economy.

THE EMERGENCE OF THE NEW BUREAUCRATIC ELITE

"The individual has little reason to fear any general laws which the majority may pass, but he has much reason to fear the rulers it may put over him to implement its direction. It is not the powers which democratic assemblies can effectively wield but the powers which they hand over to the Administrators charged with the achievement of particular goals that constitute the danger to individual freedom today."

Friedrich A. Hayek, *The Constitution of Liberty,* 1960, p. 116

Of great concern to numbers of us is the emergence of a kind of bureaucratic elite formed in this nation by government planners and politicians, large corporations, NGOs, and the academic community. While it is somewhat natural for these groups to be inter-connected simply due to their common tasks of producing leaders and strategists on higher levels, their forming of a managerial elite is certainly a threat to the exercise of choices being made freely and publicly in the democratic context of the citizenry.

In the July/August 2010 issue of *The American Spectator,* Angelo M. Codevilla wrote a very disturbing article entitled "America's Ruling Class—And the Perils of Revolution." This article is a must read for Americans who are especially concerned about the accumulation of power in a relatively small closed circle of elites. These elites have developed over the last number of decades in the academic-governmental-business world, and are rulers of substantial numbers of American institutions and governmental offices. If this article was another "scare article" it could be easily dismissed. It is not hunting for secret societies in our midst. Noting that there has always been an American elite, Codevilla writes: "Today's ruling class, from Boston to San Diego, was formed by an educational system that exposed them to the same ideas and gave them remarkably uniform guidance, as well as tastes and habits."[11] He continues, "What really distinguishes these privileged people demographically is that, whether in government power directly or as officers in companies, their careers and fortunes depend on government."[12]

President Eisenhower warned the nation in his farewell address in 1961, "The prospect of domination of the nation's scholars by Federal employment, project allocations, and the use of money is ever present and is gravely to be regarded."[13] With civil government employment growing faster recently than private sector employment, and with the massive growth in civil government over the last century, small wonder we should be concerned about this elite and its common dependency and commitment to government growth. At a time when governmental cutbacks are rapidly being made on local levels but not equally on federal levels, our nation is increasingly being set up for massive conflicts of interest between the elites and the general tax-paying citizenry. This is especially painful because the duplications of services and bureaucracies on the federal levels run into hundreds of billions of dollars annually already. A well-informed citizenry is essential to democratic freedom. How many of our citizens do you think know about this situation and its potential challenges to true choice and freedom in our nation? Have you ever heard a sermon dealing with these kinds of issues? If the church is to act as light to the nations, why isn't this happening? This economic crisis is likely going to shift this situation because it has, and will continue, to affect the jobs and lifestyles of Christians and non-Christians alike.

CHOICE, SOCIAL DARWINISM, AND THE EFFECTS OF COMPETITIVE EFFICIENCIES

Capitalism is often viewed as fatally flawed due to its competitive foundations and implications of a kind of social Darwinism producing

11. Angelo M. Codevilla, "America's Ruling Class—And the Perils of Revolution," The American Spectator, July/August 2010, 19.
12. Codevilla, 21.
13. President Dwight D. Eisenhower, *Eisenhower's Farewell Address to the Nation*, January 17, 1961.

a "survival of the fittest" social ethic. The problem with this criticism is not that it doesn't have merit, but that it leaves out other essential components of the equation. The Scriptures strike a balance between the need to add increased value to all our gifts and stewarded possessions, and the need to care for one another in the mode of community. Nowhere is competition addressed as sin per se, except in the commandments to reject greed, envy, and covetousness as an outgrowth of economic inequalities. Once again, love for our neighbors is the goal, not equality with them. Social Darwinism speaks to survival of the fittest, not the need to love one another. Capitalism as an expression of free choices is to be driven by initiative, character, and the ability to build teams of people and customers who are freely benefitting from services or products freely produced and consumed within the system. The ethical problems with capitalism are largely the result of the absence of Christian ethics influencing the system. What has amused me is the contradiction of secularists' objections to capitalism largely from those on the left, when they have attempted to eliminate Christian influences everywhere within the system.

Another major component of this issue is the question of how the choice-based market forces both competency and customer satisfaction into the economic system. Competitive efficiencies are driven by consumer choices. Eliminate consumer choices and you have not eliminated social Darwinism, you have largely eliminated the pressures of excellence and innovation from the system as well. Millions of citizens pressuring the system for value are enormously more powerful than numbers of leaders attempting to force it upon the system through programs and edicts from the top down. I personally loathe much of the banality and carnality being delivered by the current economic system, but it represents the corruption of citizens' values far more than the economic system which is only catering to their foolishness.

The power to choose brings with it the power to choose poorly and to fail. The power to choose brings both the power to exploit and the power to be indolent. Freedom is the most dangerous gift given to man as Moses noted in the beginning of this chapter. The power to choose is the power to find life and the power to bring death. Our task is not to seek to eliminate choice, but rather, to protect the less powerful from the exploitive choices of the more powerful and to bring Christ's Kingdom values to all mankind as the most reasonable of all choices available to us.

Capitalism, like all systems in a fallen world, is susceptible to grave misuse. However, contrary to many of its critics it is not primarily driven by greed or even "survival of the fittest." It is driven by man's desire to freely choose where, when, and why to invest his life energy and resources. Unfortunately, again in a fallen world, not all people within the system have equal amounts of perceived choice and part of our task is to change this. Nevertheless, capitalism as an economic system offers more elements of choice to more people than any other economic system yet to appear. Now it must be altered yet again.

POVERTY AND THE POWER OF ELEVATING OTHERS' CHOICES

"For the poor you have with you always..."
John 12:8, NKJV

Poverty will not be eliminated until Christ returns. We must diligently seek to reduce it, but rhetoric or promises to eliminate it are futile and cruel. Poverty is primarily caused by injustices within social systems, poor choices and derelictions of character, and circumstances which were pressed upon us beyond our control or ability to fully prepare for them. In this short study we will only address the question of poor choices and personal character since my comments on injustices within the system will, as they have already, continue throughout the book.

Poverty is a tragedy. It also evokes a host of different emotions. For the victims of poverty produced by injustice, it brings up anger and deep resentment. For the poor who are poor by virtue of ignorance or parental neglect, it brings up anguish and a desire to rescue the children first and then train the parents. For the poor who are poor but highly industrious, it demands from within us the need to get training and opportunities to them quickly so as to focus that industriousness into immediately fruitful activities. When we see the poor who are poor by virtue of their reliance on social systems designed by well-intentioned social workers, who are actually perpetuating that poverty by virtue of those services, it creates deep anger for a patronizing system built on subtle views of "inferior people" who need help by virtue of their class, or race, or some defect that makes the people or system providing that "care" feel good about themselves. Lastly, for the poor who feel someone else "owes" them a living, or they can simply get away with living off others' energy and finance, we often feel disgust. All of these responses and more are bundled up within the pain of poverty.

In a general sense, the left wants to leverage people out of poverty through strategic government planning and wealth redistribution. Their primary tools are taxation, quotas, and social pressure challenging economic inequalities. The right primarily focuses on free market processes and the unhindered initiative of wealthy producers providing sufficient jobs to offer pathways out of poverty and financial freedom to those willing to work for it. Both approaches, while having elements of truth within them, are obviously insufficient by virtue of the widespread existence of systemic poverty still existing even within advanced economies.

A Kingdom approach involves applying specific tools and methodologies to the specific reasons for some individuals or some people group's poverty. In terms of biblical law, that specificity required most of the list that now follows. For poverty due to social injustices, the issue is to address those injustices according to the biblical norms, making sure the economic system is operating honestly in terms of trade, currency, full disclosures, honored contracts, and most of all, a spiritually-driven commitment to honor all people as carrying the image of God and His desire to see them honored as such. For poverty due to poor parenting, the responsibility of the surrounding relatives and spiritual leaders to get involved with the parents would come into play. In terms of poverty as dealt with in the Scriptures, the mandated responsibility for the wealth producers of the economic system for the poor was to provide opportunities for gleaning (laboring for a portion of excess production as defined by the Scriptures); [14] acts of charity on a personal basis toward the poor; contracting with the poor and personally discipling

---

14. Leviticus 19:9-10.

them to create profit for themselves after fulfilling their contracts with employers;[15] and of course "the poor tax" which was collected every three years from all citizens and then distributed locally, according to personal knowledge of specific recipients of tithe money and the causes and needs of their poverty. Beyond all this were social laws on limiting all debt to seven-year terms,[16] and the fiftieth-year occurrence of jubilee.[17]

The Kingdom view of prosperity, while being relative to the needs and specific calling of each person, is built upon and driven by the desire to obey God's principles and laws of conduct and character. The world system attempts to leverage prosperity based on a system of acquiring capital or competitive advantage. The Kingdom of God leverages prosperity on the basis of faith, character, skill sets, relational skills, and most of all the ability to hear and obey the Holy Spirit's voice as He guides us in the proper application of God's Word to each and every situation or person. We believe that a transcendent God passes on resources to the obedient according to their specific roles in His Kingdom, requiring of them the stewardship of those resources in accordance with God's purposes for them. As we will further note in more detail in chapter 7, Jesus tells us in Matthew 13:12 that He redistributes wealth and resources as well, but in a way radically different from the current liberal methods that use the graduated income tax or other social devices to take from the rich and give to the poor. Jesus takes from poor stewards and gives to responsible stewards, be they rich or poor. That is why illegal gains or squandered fortunes are not rewarded in the long run by God. His remedy for poverty is good stewardship through obedient investments of energy, time, resources, charity, and compassion that invest strategic wealth-producing training in those deservedly asking for it.

POVERTY HAS ITS OWN SOCIAL SYSTEM

"An individual brings with him/her the hidden rules of the class in which he/she was raised. Even though the

15. Deuteronomy 15:12-18.
16. Exodus 22:25; Deuteronomy 15:1-2.
17. Leviticus 25.

income of the individual may rise significantly, many patterns of thought, social interaction, cognitive strategies, etc. remain with the individual. Schools and businesses operate from middle-class norms and use the hidden rules of middle class. These norms and hidden rules are not directly taught in schools or in business. For our clients to be successful, we must understand their hidden rules and teach them the rules that will make them successful at school, at work, and in the community. We can neither excuse persons from poverty nor scold them for not knowing; as professionals we must teach them and provide support, insistence, and expectations. In order to move from poverty to middle class or middle class to wealth, an individual must give up relationships for achievements (at least for some period of time)."

> Ruby K. Payne, Phillip Devol, and Terie Dreussi Smith,
> *Bridges Out of Poverty: Strategies for Professionals
> and Communities*, 2006, p. 5

I highly recommend this insightful book. It is a real eye-opener, revealing some of the deeper class and cultural issues underlining poverty. Another book of note is entitled *The Tragedy of American Compassion,* by Marvin Olasky.[18] It is well worth the read and is an excellent place to begin for those seriously interested in U.S. policies aimed at addressing poverty here in this country.

THE BIGGER PICTURE

Our immediate challenge, both here in the United States and in the other developed nations, is to address not just the issues surrounding poverty but the issues surrounding the entire collapse of our social entitlement programs on the levels now being offered. Significant numbers of our populations receive government benefits and they are not just the poor, veterans, or disabled. This situation is extremely serious as I have been attempting to communicate. This is why it offers us such an incredible opportunity to make our case for radically

---

18. Marvin Olasky, *The Tragedy of American Compassion* (Wheaton: Crossway Books, 1992).

re-examining our national values, our economic policies, our views of political freedom and the secular culture's exclusion of Christian values from our societies and the attendant costs it has brought us all. Nevertheless, all of this is in vain if the Christians of the world do not wake up and seriously engage their mandate to not just offer salvation to the people, but the blessings of freedom, prosperity, and love to their nations and social systems.

Without offering the foundational principle of choice to them, God's principles that energize these gifts will simply not function. "Choose life," Moses said.[19] We must and indeed we will if we are to both begin to move out of our current situation and advance God's Kingdom on the earth as a result. It is God's clear intent to bring true prosperity, through obedience, to all who will follow the path towards life:

"However, there will be no poor among you, since the LORD will surely bless you in the land which the LORD your God is giving you...if only you listen obediently to the voice of the LORD your God,...and you will lend to many nations, but you will not borrow;"

Deuteronomy 15:4-6

---

19. Deuteronomy 30:19.

CHAPTER 6

ON THE ECONOMIC POWER
OF GENERATIONAL MOMENTUM

"...children are not responsible to save up for their
parents, but parents for their children."

2 Corinthians 12:14

Generational momentum is like a relay race; previous generations pass on to future generations the "baton" of their wealth, knowledge, spiritual insights and stewardship skills so that every succeeding generation is starting off at the success levels of their predecessors. This is how the great dynasties of history, for good or for ill, have managed and effected history. God is the God of Abraham, Isaac, and Jacob and through this concept of three generational lines, the spiritual reality and legacy of affecting multiple generations in their lifetimes, became the goal of spiritual people who understood this pattern. The single-generational lifestyle so prevalent today, coupled with economic practices that fit it perfectly, is the underlying cause of much of this current economic crisis. Instead of laying up resources for the next generations we have stolen theirs by leaving them the debt created to support ourselves. This chapter will deal with some of the implications of that tragedy and the general demise of our prevailing views of marriage and family currently afflicting much of Western culture. It is a painful chapter to write and to read.

Nations, like people, seemingly have life spans.[1] They are birthed by necessity for survival, and grow in strength and power by the accumulation of the wealth and wisdom of the leaders and the people. Gradually, they lose their vitality as the willingness for sacrifice overcomes them and their vision for their nations' ultimate value softens into complacency. In a sense, they consume their future by living off their heritage and diminishing it for succeeding generations.

It is fair to say that we are currently at the doorstep of this condition, waiting to see if our desire for our posterity's welfare and the vitality of their nation is strong enough to give us the will and courage to pay the price to reverse the process. Without the revival—no, the compelling revival—of the passion for the welfare of our children's heritage we will surely fade into history's pattern. Why, indeed, would the Lord rescue us in our present condition of disobedience? Echoing across time I can hear the words of the prophet Malachi's indictment against a people whose fathers' hearts are separated from the hearts of their children, leaving God no alternative but to smite them with a curse—a curse of their own making.[2]

TIME IS ON THE SIDE OF
THOSE WHO THINK AND LIVE GENERATIONALLY

The great cathedrals of Europe stand as magnificent monuments to those who thought and built generationally. One generation would begin the great task of laying the huge stone foundations, and before dying, literally plant the great oak trees that their great-grandchildren would need many years later when the time for the roofs' great beams needed to be placed. This is the thinking that built many of those towering edifices. It is scarcely imaginable today. In a day of planned obsolescence the only real time we have is "right now." Seemingly, as the generation that made it through the Great Depression and World War II passes on, what we are left with in the Western world are generations whose primary vision is to maximize their own pleasures and explorations of self and whose view of leaving a meaningful future

---

1. Acts 17:26.
2. Malachi 4:4-6.

for others is seldom an issue of public discussion. Only recently in the context of this economic crisis have such ideas become public again and primarily from conservatives as an indictment against the left.

Those critics of traditional society, who set out to deconstruct it, used no weapon more powerful than to ridicule and destroy the validity of the idea of children opting to join the life vision and values of their parents. The concept of children joining in any kind of cathedral endeavor with their parents,[3] traversing generations with some grand project or even one simply buried in the hearts of their parents, became grounds for crying "parental control," or the cruel need for one generation to superimpose their own opinions upon another. Only the business corporation was allowed to build across generations without censure. Even the national political process became the target of deconstructionists. A nation's constitution must not superimpose the dictates of the founders' values or theories of government unduly upon future generations. Generational transfer, as a concept, must be swept away and replaced by the demand that the inheritance of values be handled with the utmost of care laced with suspicion. "Control" became the new Satan and the target of those demanding to become free.

To the single-generational thinkers and builders, time is a bit of an enemy. Indeed, no project can or should necessarily be passed across one generation and imposed upon another. The existential view of creating value for the "right now" has made history virtually irrelevant and the future of value only to those who will be there. To the biblical followers of Christ, any vision which can be fully achieved within one lifetime is probably too small. For us time is on our side. The great drama of God's unrolling of time, as the wave carrying His purposes, is a song built by every generation as it carries the theme of God's triumphant Kingdom. It energizes His people, gaining momentum with every generation as it builds upon the revelations of God's triumphant Kingdom. For us, a generation that lives for itself interrupts the momentum of the wave and makes its recovery difficult. This is where we stand today. We need multiple thousands of pulpits around the world challenging parents and children to join their lives and purposes

---

3.   1 Chronicles 22:1-16.

together, not doing the exact same things, but committed to the same heart for God's Kingdom purposes as it keeps the relay race going and the passing of the same baton from each generation to the next.

JOHN MAYNARD KEYNES:
THE ECONOMIST MOST RESPONSIBLE FOR STOPPING THE RELAY

It is difficult to point to any major public figure of the twentieth century with a greater effect on stopping the concept of generational thinking than the brilliant economist, John Maynard Keynes. Keynes's economic theories have had the greatest influence on modern economic theory and the establishing of contemporary economic practices. He emerged as the world systems' "answer" to the economic crisis of the Great Depression and defined economic theory in the West at least as much as Marx had done in the socialist world. His *General Theory of Employment, Interest and Money*, published in 1936, set the tone for liberalism's view of economic practices up to the present day.[4] In spite of the Chicago School of economics' refutations (based on the work of Von Mises and Hayek), this view of the aggressive role of civil government in the management of the economy has largely led the day until now.

Keynes's economic theories on governmental monetary and fiscal policies carried a shockingly cavalier attitude regarding their likely effect on future generations. Essentially, his policies demanded certain levels of consumption and governmental spending that required inflationary additions to the money supply, insuring that governmental debt would be the inevitable result as it passed one generation's debt burdens on to the next. This is exactly what eventually has happened as the "me first" values of the "sixties" took a firmer grip on the leadership of those in governmental power from the 1970s onward. More restrained views on the issues of government debt grew weaker and weaker. When confronted with this highly likely possibility of massive debt cumulatively taking place, Keynes's retort was "In the long run we are

4.   John Maynard Keynes, *General Theory of Employment, Interest, and Money* (London: Macmillan and Co., Ltd., 1936).

all dead."[5] This is economic lingo for saying, "Whatever happens to future generations based on current generation's perceived spending needs is their problem." It also demonstrates extreme inconsideration for parents as providers and role models for their children.

In addition, Keynes led a group of deconstructionist leaders connected with Cambridge University who called themselves "the Apostles". He was openly homosexual and strongly committed to spreading the virtues of his orientation. He kept diaries of his forays and belonged to the Bloomsbury Group, whose members were known for their similarly freewheeling attitudes and lifestyles. I am citing this not out of moral concerns in this discussion, but rather out of the obvious effects his orientation had on his view of economic theory. He clearly cared very little for future generations, based on the debt levels he was willing to create for them by borrowing from them for the current generations, hoping to create added employment through government spending or higher levels of consumption to stimulate the economy. The point of these effects relative to his sexual orientation was that his parental concerns or views regarding children were non-existent in his conversations, and his books featured strong attacks on the "traditional life-styles" as he called them, of traditional society and traditional family morals.

Some may say that I am stretching the issues of his preferences too far here. After more than forty years of personal counseling of people, I don't think so. People's worldview and moral and ethical values directly or indirectly show up in virtually all they do and say, and especially in their theoretical views of life.[6] From a biblical point of view our morality affects our ability to hear God and practice truth. From an economic point of view, how we allocate resources is clearly determined by our priorities—how current actions will affect future results—and Keynes was no fool. He knew the long-term implications of what he was advocating.

---

5. John Maynard Keynes, *A Tract on Monetary Reform* (London: Macmillan and Co., Ltd., 1923), 80.
6. Matthew 13:14-15.

HOW GENERATIONAL MOMENTUM WORKS

Generational thinking or momentum begins with the health of parents' hearts. Do they love their children enough to train them to succeed in life or is that too much trouble? If they don't, or haven't been trained by their own parents on how to do so,[7] they need to get help. So where does that help come from? From a Christian point of view, it comes from their spiritual leaders. Now the hard news: it isn't usually that simple.

The non-Christian world is filled with parental paralysis. Very, very few parents know how to train their children; very few parents even know if the act of training children is permissible without becoming controlling or invasive. Remember, for them, the relay race idea is commonly viewed as a very self-centered and non-loving act. If their parents demonstrated clear parental training they were in a very small minority in modern Western culture. It is hard to blame people for ignorance. It is not hard to challenge them to get help. Our pain is that we Christians have exported so little of what truth we do have in these areas. Here we are again back at our main problem; we have invested primarily in ourselves rather than adding our truth to our surrounding cultures.

So let us give some clear ideas on the things that generational momentum training does in terms of the stewardship side of life. First, we are to train our children to train. That means we teach and model for them the reality that virtue and excellence require work, training, and time to perfect itself in order to become a habit. Letting things "happen" is a wonderful way to be ruled by circumstances instead of helping to shape outcomes. We usually hit what we aim for when our aim is realistic and undergirded by effort and character. The Scriptures say "train up a child,"[8] not give them guidance or suggestions. If that sounds too rigid, then please do not expect your children to achieve mastery in any particular area in spite of their natural abilities.

Second, we must give the concept and reality of generational momentum to our children and grandchildren. They must see the obvious advantage

---

7.   Proverbs 6:20-23.
8.   Proverbs 22:6.

to them and their children of inheriting now, as well as later, the skill sets and resources of their parents as they go through life.[9] While it is quite true that we should properly relate to our children based upon their age and training levels, gradually releasing more and more power and authority to them as they mature, we should still stay intimately connected with their hearts and the common goals we have for our family's future as they create families of their own. Generational momentum or transfer is an exciting adventure across time wherein the death of one generation simply springboards the next one.

Third, we should be searching with them, and solidifying what we already have discerned, about special callings or gifts that God has placed within our families. All that God creates has design. This is true for individuals, families, organizations, and nations. Generational momentum is not just about accumulating power or position through asset management; it is about discovering and enhancing the callings and gifts resident within family members relative to Kingdom work which they are called to do across the generations. God shows us this pattern in the way He works in Scripture through family lines. Iniquities and negative tendencies clearly pass from generation to generation.[10] Are we to believe that blessings and callings do not pass along as well? It is no accident that Jesus came through the kingly line of David. Beginning with Adam and then Abraham, God implants His purposes and His prophetic callings through family lines. How sad it is that so few families are aware of this to be able to live it out. Very sad, and more than that, how much have we all been robbed in terms of benefits because these resident gifts were never released or magnified?

We could talk about family training in the areas of conflict resolution skills, communication skills, marriage skills or a long list of other skills which most people discover the hard way in life. However, we need to move on to another of the really large economically related skills required to energize generational momentum. I am talking about stewardship skills, the ability to care for and enhance the value of material or relational gifts entrusted to us by God.

---

9. Proverbs 13:22.
10. Exodus 20:5-6.

What now follows is one of the most challenging spiritual laws I am aware of, one that initially contradicts our whole sense of fair play or human need until we see God's point of view:

> "For whoever has, to him more shall be given, and he
> will have an abundance; but whoever does not have,
> even what he has shall be taken away from him."
>
> Matthew 13:12

This challenging principle should be engraved on every government building in the world, and upon the front door into every economic professor's classroom in the academic community. God owns all things and therefore whatever we have is on loan in a stewardship trust with and for Him. The principle works this way: Whoever cares for and brings added value to their stewardship possessions will be entrusted with more things and even more relational or leadership responsibilities than they are currently managing. If the common adage "use it or lose it" carries truth, and it does, we can biblically say, "Bring care and value to it or you will lose it and other things you are not adequately caring for as well."

The Scriptures say that wealth quickly gained cannot be held for long.[11] Why? Because the skill sets required to manage it correctly are not there. How many stories about lottery winners do we need to hear to believe this? How about professional athletes coming from poverty into millions of dollars and then retiring or getting injured only to be flat broke soon afterward? Riches that are kept, let alone passed on through generational momentum are kept and added to because the wisdom to manage them was passed on prior to their receiving these assets.

Part of the great pain I am experiencing because of this economic crisis is the damage being done to marriages and people's self-worth due to prolonged unemployment, or the loss of millions of private homes due to mortgage foreclosure. The economic spin-offs from this are severely damaging the construction industries, realty markets, and all the durable goods related to those vital industries. Trillions of dollars

---

11. Proverbs 20:21; 28:20.

of savings have been lost to American home owners as the housing bubble burst. This deflation left middle class Americans defunded and separated from years of the fruits of their labor and savings. The banks have fared far better.

God honors people who upgrade their stewardship skills. The success stories of sacrifice, time investment, and relational investments are not just stories for the strong, the empowered ethnic groups, or anyone else who is "special". They are for all of us in every generation, ethnic group, or vocation. God and man honor diligence and will invest in it when they recognize it. Stewardship is an issue of choice, not class, skin color, or even the level of current possessions. From Mexico and Central America to Africa, from East L.A. to Eastern Europe and beyond, I have personally observed numerous poor people caring industriously for what they have. They are not more loved by God necessarily for doing so but they are virtually always rewarded with more power, privilege, and respect within their economic context. Frequently, they are the first to exit from the condition of their poverty.

The Kingdom parable of good stewardship being rewarded and poor stewardship being punished is well known to all students of the Scriptures. Matthew 25:1-30 begins with the story of the ten virgins and then proceeds to the story of a master going on a journey and dispensing his money to three of his servants. In Luke 19:11-27, the message is similar but the reward for good stewardship is the rulership over cities rather than simply a wealth transfer from the master to his servants. In the cases of the currencies given to the servants, Jesus praised the investors and rebuked the stewards who did not even have the good sense to put the money in the bank and receive interest. How interesting it is that Jesus did not negatively comment on either banking or charging interest, but recognized that wise investments are obviously more lucrative. In both cases the poor stewards were defunded and in the Matthew text, they were exiled from the master's presence.[12]

In the remainder of Matthew 25, Jesus gives us an excellent teaching on the principle of care and charity. As He separates the nations as

---

12. Matthew 25:30.

"sheep and goats,"[13] He reminds us in the overall context of this chapter that one needs resources (stewardship) in order to give away charity. We cannot give away what we do not have.

Let us move on now from the issues of generational momentum and move to a much more sobering topic greatly affecting the economic welfare of many nations. While these issues we are about to touch on carry immense social and ethical consequences, we will look at them, for the sake of this study, primarily from an economic point of view.

THE TRAGEDY OF CURRENT U.S. ECONOMIC FAMILY POLICIES

As we have noted before, at its core, economics is primarily about values and secondarily about the computations required to give us information related to the economic applications of those values. An economic transaction takes place, based on a values choice, and we then measure its effect based on the information we are looking at. When we are talking economic data of any kind we are actually looking at values choices that have been made within the marketplace context. The current economic crisis tells us that significant values choices have been going on for some time and they are now showing up as a "crisis" based on their cumulative effects on the economic and social systems. Understanding these things is essential to our ability to understand that we must first change our values in order to produce economic changes that reflect those values choices. In short, we cannot fix our economy until we first change the values that sent it into a crisis. Please remember this.

The traditional family unit has historically been viewed as the core social unit of any culture or economy. The family unit, for good or ill, is the first engine of social values that we have as children. This is why healthy nations or healthy economies are built on healthy family units producing wise decision makers who create solid economic markets. Unfortunately, we seldom ever hear this level of reality from social leaders or economists. We are deep enough now into the more economically focused discussions of this book to reiterate these things more specifically.

---

13. Matthew 25:32-33.

We can convincingly say from the data that measures healthy family indicators such as divorce rates, child and spousal abuse, abortion and out-of-wedlock birth rates, pornography, crime rates and imprisonments, substance abuse and other, similar social indicators that the strength of the traditional family unit has greatly diminished the last fifty years. Since all of these values shifts have both direct and indirect economic consequences, what we will now discuss should be of particular interest to anyone attempting to offer policy remedies to our economic crisis. For us as believers the biblical anchor to the social and economic health of any nation is that strong marriages produce healthy families. It is the very foundation of God's covenant with His people through our father of the faith:

> "'And I will bless those who bless you (Abraham),
> And the one who curses you I will curse. And in you
> all the families of the earth will be blessed.'"
>
> Genesis 12:3

THE GROWING DEMISE OF COVENANT MARRIAGE IN WESTERN CULTURE

> "For this reason a man shall leave his father and his mother, and be joined to his wife; and they shall become one flesh."
>
> Genesis 2:24

God is the One who instituted human marriage and its covenant nature. Man may alter it to suit his desires but it is no longer a marriage in the context in which God established it. The State can call any other form of "marriage" whatever they want but it is fundamentally different than a Judeo-Christian institution. In terms of our marriages, it may well prove to have been a major mistake for the Church to have ever allowed the State's involvement in any form. Be that as it may, the shifts in traditional marriages are one of the largest changes in Western civilization since the fall of the Roman Empire.

Marriage, until relatively recently, was viewed as a covenant and not simply a legal contract. The State regulates legal contracts but it actually has no power before God to involve itself in a covenantal issue between believers, and covenantal marriage is therefore truly a church matter and only involves the State because the State reached into the church's domain and became a regulator. Obviously, when the Christian-based cultures of the Western world approved of the State's involvement in the institution of marriage they never anticipated the complete secularization of the process by the State.

God has set forth the conditions of marriage in the Scriptures and Jesus both reiterated His support for the institution of marriage and the only terms Scripture gives for its dissolution. Marriage therefore has an institutional dimension to it that both defines its purposes and terms, and has the power of God within it to grace people with the ability to live out a marriage successfully. Dietrich Bonhoeffer, the noted Christian theologian martyred by Hitler, stated the matter clearly: "It is not your love that sustains the marriage, but from now on, the marriage that sustains your love."[14] The covenant itself has power within it.

This view of marriage rapidly began to break down in the Western world after World War II. As it did, it created massive changes in cultures sociologically, economically, and demographically. Sociologically, the government began to grant "no-fault divorces," making marriage the only legal contract that could be broken by either side with impunity. Divorce became both easy and without social stigma. This resulted in massive divorces, remarriages, and split homes. The effects on children became well documented, including: insecurity, anger, guilt, and a challenge to believe in the permanence of relationships. Economically, the social fragmentation of the family resulted in massive amounts of governmental expenditures to care for the social debris. This included aid to dependent children, care facilities of all kinds, the skyrocketing costs related to out-of-wedlock births, and the social challenges related to increases in crime, incarceration, and loss of income caused by increased drop-out rates in schools.

When the family unit does not adequately train the children to succeed in life, some other social unit takes up that cost. That cost is not only in

---

14. Dietrich Bonhoeffer, *Letters and Papers from Prison*, rev. ed., ed. Eberhard Bethge (New York: Macmillan, 1967), 27-28.

economic terms, it has emotional and psychological terms as well. New nurturing and support systems must be established, even though they frequently prove to be no emotional substitute for a functioning natural family. Fragmented families cost the United States billions of dollars annually as the following quote and its supporting data amply show:

> "Based upon the methodology, we estimate that family fragmentation costs the U.S. taxpayers at least $112 billion each and every year, or more than $1 trillion each decade. These costs are arising from increased taxpayer expenditures for antipoverty, criminal justice, and educational programs, and through lower levels of taxes paid by individuals who, as adults, earn less because of reduced opportunities as a result of having been more likely to grow up in poverty...The $112 billion figure represents a 'lower bound' or minimum estimate."

Benjamin Scafidi, Principal Investigator,
"Taxpayer Costs of Divorce and Unwed Childbearing,"
Executive Summary, The Institute for American Values, 2008

THE DEMOGRAPHICS OF THE DEMISE OF FAMILY VALUES

Demographically, family fragmentation has produced a dramatic drop in birth rates of most Western nations as well. This has produced a significant rise in foreign immigration which has brought about some of its own complications, due to the social systems required to support many immigrants and the cultural challenges coming from religious and ethnic dissimilarities, especially in a number of the European countries undergoing these migrations.

The Death of the West by Pat Buchanan deals with the demographics of the effects of this radical change in family values in terms of decreasing populations. The numbers occurring in many of the European nations are frightening. These ominous figures have major economic implications which we will shortly discuss.

> "The West is dying. Its nations have ceased to reproduce, and their populations have stopped growing and begun

to shrink. Not since the Black Death carried off a third of Europe in the fourteenth century has there been a graver threat to the survival of Western civilization."

Pat Buchanan, *The Death of the West*, 2002, p. 19

This is the first time in history that an indigenous population has voluntarily become a minority rather than through war, famine or disease.

The Death of the West is not a prediction of what is going to happen. It is already happening. "At present birthrates, Europe must bring in 169 million immigrants by 2050 if it wishes to keep its population aged fifteen to sixty-four at today's levels. But if Europe wishes to keep its present *ratio* of workers (fifteen—sixty-four) for every senior, Europe must bring in *1.4 billion* immigrants from Africa and the Middle East."[15] How I wish these numbers were not true, but I am not aware of a credible refutation of Pat's researched numbers.

Even a short analysis of the economic implications of Europe's population issues tells us that with their current massive debts and a number of EU nations already insolvent, the European economy will continue to have a major negative effect on the financial health and markets of the whole world. In today's "flat" world of intertwined financial systems and labor markets, there is no such thing as a truly protected nation in terms of today's lifestyle levels. A shrinking population, or a population where immigrants are replacing the traditionally higher income rates of indigenous retirees or those lost through death, it is clear that government revenue through taxation will go down and the cost of supporting the immigrants will go up. These are the kinds of problems with which the new leaders will have to deal.

Here in the U.S., our birth rate is slightly below the 2.2 percent replacement level of births required to maintain current populations.[16] Our immigration levels from Mexico and beyond have helped maintain

---

15. Pat Buchanan, *The Death of the West* (New York: St. Martin's Press, 2002), 22.
16. Laura B. Shrestha and Elayne J. Heisler, *The Changing Demographic Profile of the United States,* (Washington, DC: Congressional Research Service, September 25, 2009), 5. http://aging.senate.gov/crs/aging4.pdf.

our gradual growth in recent years. All of this immigration is obviously not without its own set of economic challenges. In California, it is estimated that illegal immigrants cost the state more than $11 billion annually in net social services expenses.[17] While it is beyond the scope of this book to deal with the comprehensive solutions to these immigrant issues, they are surely affecting our national social systems negatively from an economic point of view.

Japan is depopulating at a rate that can only be called tragic.[18] This is especially true since prior to World War II, the family unit was the centering point of their social systems and religious focus. Once fully exposed to the West, they have reversed their historic place for the family. Japan has been a major source of funding for the U.S. debt and clearly their ability or will to do so is going to dramatically change. Even China, based on its one-child government policies, will begin to experience a shrinking population in the coming years. All of the above information is filled with mostly negative consequences relative to current economic conditions. And now the really tough one....

THE ECONOMIC CONSEQUENCES OF ABORTION

Dealing with abortion is a most difficult issue, especially in terms of economic consequences, because we are talking about innocent human beings here and not just economic figures. Nevertheless, we must do so because the economic consequences of abortion are horrific, like everything else surrounding the termination of these millions and millions of lives. I can well imagine God saying to the nations who have practiced this incomprehensible policy, "OK, you could not hear the moral side of this issue, so let's see what you think of the economic consequences it will have on your precious 'lifestyle' needs." So let's talk about the economic ramifications of abortion for the United States which, as the world's largest economy, will have obvious effects on the rest of the world also.

17. "The Costs of Illegal Immigration to Californians," Washington, DC: FAIR, 2004.
18. Blaine Harden, "Born in Japan, But Ordered Out," *Washington Post*, January 17, 2010. http://www.washingtonpost.com/wp-dyn/content/article/2010/01/16/AR2010011602639.html.

In a significant section of our population, children are seen as an impediment to freedom and lifestyle choices, so they must be aborted. Historically, they have been seen as the hope for the future, a blessing, and a means of perpetuating our own lives across time. That is surely how the Scriptures see them as do those who are practicing economic momentum in their families now.

The United States has aborted somewhere between 50 and 60 million children over the last forty years depending on whose figures you believe. Currently the figures are about 1.2 million per year.[19] Approximately 13 million of them were African Americans, which represents a number nearly 2.5 times the total number of deaths caused in this community over the same period of time for all other deaths caused by AIDS, cancer, accidents, heart disease, and violent crime combined.[20] Clearly, Planned Parenthood, the organization formed by its racist white founder has done a good job of fulfilling its original purposes. Congratulations, Margret Sanger. I am sure hell is clapping.

Let us break down what these kinds of numbers really mean from an economic perspective. Let us assume a mid-range number of total abortions to be 55 million. To put this number in perspective this is the equivalent of killing nearly all the current population of Great Britain, and not that far from killing most of France. It is far more than all who died globally in World War II, and nearly ten times more than all our casualties in the Vietnam War. It is more than 110 times all the people who went to Woodstock, for those of you who may have done so. We abort more than ten of our largest football stadiums (100,000) full of babies every year.

Let us assume that the ones aborted from 1973 to 1983 are now 29 to 39 years old. How many of these multiple millions would have had children by now? I would say at least half of them would have one or more children based on current numbers. The ones aborted between 1983 and 1993 would now be 18 to 28 years old. Many of them would have been married. The ones born from 1994 until now would be 17 or

19. Lynn Vincent, "Black Genocide," World Magazine, January 17, 2009, 36.
20. Ibid.

younger. They would be happily in school for the most part or at least about to enter school. Assuming 1.3 million abortions for the earlier years, to be conservative, since the numbers grew quickly and peaked some years ago, the first group of 29 to 39 would number about 13 million and would have worked for a number of years, paying taxes of course. The next group takes up to about 30 million total (these were the heaviest years of abortion), and most of them would be employed and paying taxes. So how much tax revenue have we lost from these 30 million workers over the various tenures of their employment? Hundreds of millions for sure.

Let's go in another direction. How many doctors and professionals were in this group? How many additional houses do we need for these 55 million people? How about teachers and schools? How many pants, shirts, skirts, and blouses do 50 million people need every year? We have surely hundreds of millions of shoes and socks. Try adding your items to the list and think about how many millions of this or that our economy lost in terms of production, jobs, local tax revenues, and the like.

How many workers from these 55 million would have been gainfully employed over the next fifty or so years to help pay for the retirement benefits and health care needs of the parents who aborted them? When Social Security was inaugurated in the United States in the 1930s, the ratio of workers to retirees was about 37:1. Now, after these abortions it is nearing seven or eight to one and some say it is going down to less than five to one. Folks, we are talking about having removed nearly one-fifth of our entire population of 300 million people. Just think of all the so-called economic multiplier effects of economic activity they would currently be generating if we were in fact the 350 million strong we would be, with them here.

I do not have the heart to further address the complications these abortions have brought to us. Nor will I deal with the tragedies of other dimensions of our social policies dealing with the inner cities, and the plight of a society where seven out of ten African American children are born out of wedlock and 30 percent of fatherless black men in America go to jail. The human and economic consequences of it all are too much to take in.

SOME FINAL THOUGHTS

Generational momentum is part of the major solution to all these problems. We desperately need functioning fathers and mothers, bound in functioning families where their children are the first and greatest responsibility of their parents. We need national policies that see generational momentum as one of, if not the first order of our economic priorities. Out from such nations would come leaders and people who in several generations would be changing the entire planet. If we love our children we should give them the advantage of living their lives on our shoulders or beyond, so to speak. A nation that loves its families loves its future. Parentally speaking, this is the outworking of Christ's greatest commandment and a centerfold of an enlightened economic policy.

CHAPTER 7

ON CONNECTING CAPITAL CREATION
WITH EMPLOYMENT INCENTIVES

The laws of the land can force changes in behavior, but they cannot change the hearts of the people.[1] This is the work of the Holy Spirit, and it is suicidal for any nation to attempt to exclude His presence from His people's culture, nation, or economic policies. This chapter reaches out for the ways in which economic intentions can more fully direct the hearts of capital producers toward a social ethic of full employment, with living wages for the greatest number of people.

ON THE NATURE OF CAPITAL: AN OVERVIEW

Capital is unspent resource available and directed toward the production of profit from an economic venture. While we can also speak easily of different kinds of capital such as capital assets, relational capital, intellectual capital, etc., in this discussion I am directing the meaning of capital toward the ability to create new resources through new capital investments. Capital, wisely invested and managed, produces not only new capital but employment, new consumption rates, added taxation income, and a host of other related economic benefits and outcomes. Capital investments, through either the private sector directly or, indirectly from the government investing capital from taxation revenues, are what stimulate economic growth in multiple ways.

---

1. Ezekiel 36:26.

Capital investments are the lifeblood of any growing economy and are essential to keep up with any healthy population growth and the need to offer new citizens gainful employment.

Capital formation, as all of you know, is directly related to savings rates and the willingness to defer or postpone consumption of disposable income, instead directing it toward the production of more capital. All of what I just said is once again a set of values-related choices determined by the individual but affected by our social environments. Hence, economics comes back again to the question of who is influencing the social-spiritual environment of the culture and the nation in question. Now we are back to "square one" so to speak, which is the issue of discipling nations and therefore both directly and indirectly affecting their economic policies and outcomes. To leave all of this to secular forces or any other spiritual forces is not only spiritually disobedient but economically self-destructive to the church and our own needs for gainful employment and the resources to invest in an expanding Kingdom.

The questions then arise: Why is the church largely absent from its post as a discipler of nations (because of dualism, ignorance, and complacency)? What can and should be done to stimulate appropriate savings rates in a nation so as to create capital investments, jobs, and lifestyles built on Kingdom values? That is where we must now go. Indeed, what are the principles that stimulate or hinder accelerating capital formation rates and the growth of both employment and the general economy?

JESUS TEACHES ON THE VALUE OF EMPLOYMENT

The Scriptures tell us that God's ways are higher than our ways and He thinks on very different levels than we think.[2] We have already noted several examples of this, most poignantly Matthew 13:12, where we see Jesus taking from the poor stewards and giving to the rich stewards. His economic class-transfers are going in the wrong direction according to virtually everything we have been taught in economics or civics classes! Now, we are about to see another example of Jesus not

---

2. Isaiah 55:8-9.

just thinking out of the box, but redefining what the boxes themselves should be.

> "[1]'For the kingdom of heaven is like a landowner who went out early in the morning to hire laborers for his vineyard. [2] When he had agreed with the laborers for a denarius for the day, he sent them into his vineyard. [3] And he went out about the third hour and saw others standing idle in the market place; [4] and to those he said, "You also go into the vineyard, and whatever is right I will give you." And so they went. [5] Again he went out about the sixth and ninth hour, and did the same thing. [6] And about the eleventh hour he went out, and found others standing around; and he said to them, "Why have you been standing here idle all day long?"[7] They said to him, "Because no one hired us." He said to them, "You go into the vineyard too."[8] 'When evening came, the owner of the vineyard said to his foreman, "Call the laborers and pay them their wages, beginning with the last group to the first."'[9] When those hired about the eleventh hour came, each one received a denarius. [10] When those hired first came, they thought they would receive more; but each of them also received a denarius. [11] When they received it, they grumbled at the landowner,[12] saying, "These last men have worked only one hour, and you have made them equal to us who have borne the burden and the scorching heat of the day."[13] But he answered and said to one of them, "Friend, am I doing you no wrong; did you not agree with me for a denarius?[14] Take what is yours and go your way, but I wish to give to this last man the same as to you.[15] Is it not lawful for me to do what I wish with my own? Or is your eye envious because I am generous?[16] So the last shall be first, and the first last."'

Matthew 20:1-16

There are many lessons here as with all of Jesus' parables, but we will focus on several specific ones related to our task at hand. Our first reaction to His obvious economic "injustice" is to observe how patently "unfair" this Kingdom of God must be. How, pray tell, can Jesus be advocating such unfair wage practices? These workers need a union and the landowner needs a good punitive labor violations fine. So it would seem to most of us raised and educated in the modern Western world of enlightened social values.

However, as is usually the case, perspective is everything. Let us first deal with some of the more obvious concerns:

1. Does the landowner have the right to do whatever he lawfully wants with his own possessions? Yes.

2. Did he and his laborers have clear wage agreements prior to their services rendered? Evidently, since no one made claims to the contrary.

3. Were the laborers' services acceptable to the landowner? Yes, according to the story.

4. Did the landowner agree that the first hired worked longer than the last hired? Yes, clearly.

So in what way does this supposedly "unfair" story give us any helpful insight into the Kingdom of God, save do not be surprised if your harder labor goes unrewarded relative to others' lesser input? Now, we are perhaps ready for the lessons at hand.

Firstly, there is not a single word about the landowner's concern for either his crop or its value. As a Kingdom steward I have no doubt he cared about both of those things, and Jesus clearly did based on the emphasis He commonly placed on stewardship in His other parables. But here, nary a word. Secondly, there is no indication here of any concerns being expressed regarding negotiations of wages. The expectations of the earlier laborers for higher wages were not unreasonable but clearly the *denarius* was for the whole day's wages and was not a by-the-hour wage agreement. So what is the critical point of Jesus' parable?

For me, it is this: The landowner could not stand to see unemployed laborers standing idle in the marketplace when they could be gainfully employed and experiencing the dignity of work and the ability to provide for themselves and the needs of others. He so hated that possibility that he went out early in the morning and four more times right up until the end of the day to prevent it. God cares deeply about wasted skill sets; He is deeply concerned for the souls of men and women who languish because they are "unhired," idling in the depression of not being able to reveal their creativity, courage, or tangible proof that they are worth being hired and valued for who they are. Of all the multiple tragedies on the earth, few are more personally debilitating than the feeling of being unused by God or man. It eats at the soul and devours one's sense of self-worth. Either in the church or in the marketplace, being relevant and usable for who we are and who we are becoming is at the core of human dignity.

As one who deals with "the economic and social sides of these things," my heart is broken for the unhired, the unemployed, and underemployed. This may be "economics" to others, but to me it is about the dignity and value of humanity. I think I get what Jesus' parable is about here: God's passion to impart value to all and irrelevance to none. When I hear about the millions of mortgage failures, with millions more on the way, I know behind each and every one of them is a sense of failure and a loss of dignity or hope for those who once had the joy, many of them for the first time, of owning their own homes. When I learn something about manipulated and inaccurate statistics being given to us concerning unemployment numbers, or I see the latest figures, these are not just numbers to me. They are unfulfilled lives, men and women facing the challenges of being unable to provide for themselves or others and experiencing the declining challenge of believing in their own self-worth. Economics indeed must measure things but those "things" are ultimately about real people's lives.

VALUES AND PRINCIPLES THAT STIMULATE CAPITAL INVESTMENTS

So, what then is our task? It is far more than economic growth, though it is about that to be sure. It is about maximizing gainful employment and stimulating that desire in the maximum number of capital creators and government policy setters as is possible. To say that such an idea is impossible or impractical in a capitalistic system is absurd. Capitalism is subject to the values of its participants, and the fable of all things going to the lowest bidders or those maximizing the cheapest production costs is just that, a fable.

The marketplace rewards excellence, reputation, and above all the ability to identify with someone or some cause that allows the purchaser of goods or services to feel part of the perceived ethic or value of the producers. If this were not true, then why would the advertising world spend multi-billions of dollars annually attempting to brand their products or services with specific values or purchaser identifying marks? The lowest cost pricing takes only a share of the capitalistic world market, and far from all of it, especially in the values-sensitive Western markets. Prestige and honor triumph the lowest cost in even the lowest economic sectors. Have you checked out what brands are selling hottest among youth of our inner cities? I can assure you that it is not the lowest cost items in the market. It is the same for the middle classes on up. I rest my case. Capitalism sells prestige and "belonging" as much as the lowest price. We can change the way the capital creators view their mission, or Jesus would not have wasted His time on a parable He knew would go out to billions of people over time. It is all about getting a Kingdom perspective.

THE GOVERNMENT'S ROLE

In my lifetime, which spans twelve U.S. presidents, I cannot remember hearing a single president clearly explaining the relationship between taxation policies, capital creation, and employment to the American people. How is that possible? I am sure that it may have happened and I missed the event, but it is such a critical thing that one might expect to hear such an explanation on a regular basis, particularly since the public is so driven by concern for economic health in their nation. Do high school civics classes deal with such things? I am also fairly certain that, beyond the finance or economics majors, few college students could intelligently discuss this issue. Once again, since economics drives many if not most elections according to years of poll taking, why is such a basic and important topic not commonly understood by the voting public of so many nations?

Reiterating what most of you know well, socialism believes that a government planned economy has the best chance of producing a stable economy for the overall community of citizens. Capitalism believes that free market mechanisms run much more effectively than a governmentally planned economy, and a free market system produces a larger middle class quickly with upward economic mobility for the most people, in spite of the system's economic inequalities. Today, the world's economies are largely mixed, with varying degrees of State planning and market regulations. We have already raised the issues of so-called government interventions and unintended consequences so we will not go there in any depth again. What I will say is that while the government can regulate economic activities and invest in job creation it cannot inspire people to save and create capital for the outworking of a personal vision. That passion comes from the heart, not the government, and that reality alone explains why the more free market economies of the world out-produce any governmentally focused economic system.

The government sector can create jobs but it cannot directly create capital. Government jobs create public liabilities because government jobs, as necessary as they may be, must be paid through raising sufficient taxes to pay for the creation of new jobs. It is true that government contracts to the private sector create income in the private sector to offset those increased taxes, but job creation in the private sector is undoubtedly the fastest and most direct way to create capital. A recent example of this quest for government stimulation of the economy and its sometimes serious inefficiencies is the expenditures of so-called TARP (troubled asset relief program) funds designed to create jobs here in the U.S. The stimulus money did create new jobs but at a price of $275,000 per job according to numerous surveys. While grateful for all the jobs that were created, the question remains: Was this the most efficient way to do it? I think not. Some familiar with economics may point to the so-called multiplier effects which economically spun off from these jobs as very significant but numbers of studies have shown that those multiplier effects are generally far less than we were academically taught to expect.

> "It is difficult to be productive when government restrictions hamper the pooling of resources, when taxes and tariffs distort the price of materials and products, and when price controls distort production incentives. The same is true when red tape, including accounting requirements and other procedural rules, increase costs and when labor laws render the mobility of labor virtually impossible, making it extremely costly to engage new staff."
>
> Hernando DeSoto, *The Other Path*, 2002, p. 173

DeSoto's comments are a veritable laundry list of complaints against undue government interference in the private sector and are aimed at the challenges of doing business in an emerging economy. However, all those elements exist to varying degrees in all the economies of the world. While it is very easy to get "amens" from the business community when these issues of undue government interference are brought up, my own view is that until the business community regulates itself more thoroughly, the government will do it for them and much more ineffectively and restrictively. This current global reordering is a clear example of what happens when the private sector and the government sector both cast off restraint in an effort to experience quick money on high risk investments, from artificial markets, using absurdly low interest rates to loan money to unqualified people. Where was the regulation of both the private and public sectors there? Greed, ineffective financial regulation, and political expediency gave us the "perfect financial storm."

What I am saying is that in a fallen world, laws and regulations are essential.[3] However, the rule of thumb is the more internal self-government the citizenry has, the less external laws and regulations are necessary. I am quite sure history proves that axiom to be true.

---

3. 1 Timothy 1:8-9.

In fact, that idea is the very foundation of child rearing, wherein children gain more and more freedom and less and less restrictions by demonstrating responsible actions. What parent, or enlightened politician for that matter, can argue with that reality? Obviously, undue regulations hinder the formation of new capital and stifle economic growth by making sure the expenditures of new investments of time, energy, and money are not worth investing in, due to the restrictions placed on those who would otherwise make them. So when do we best regulate? When the most ethical and responsible leaders of any given industry or service are clear that some current practices are endangering a fair and level playing field or endangering the general welfare of the citizenry.

The apostle Paul encouraged believers to set up their own courts to deal with the Christian community's own regulatory issues.[4] I would love to see the church come to the place where we were mature enough to do so. But until then, the least we can do is exert a strong moral presence in the marketplace and beyond and minimize the needs for laws and general regulations because of the salutary effects we are having on our local communities and nations. That is truly "net-fishing evangelism" and an obvious way to disciple nations in a clear and measurable fashion. I have maintained for years that one can tell a great deal about a nation's general moral direction by the amount of new laws emerging yearly. For my U.S. fellow citizens, I urge you to look it up and see for yourselves how many new laws annually are enacted here in Congress. Prepare for a shock.

Simply put, undue regulations and taxation levels that cause a serious drop in investments create slowed down economies, the constricting of available money for business operations and loans of all kinds, and the resultant loss of jobs. The art of economics then becomes the ability to correctly answer this question: What regulations are "undue" and how much taxation on what activities will chase too many capital investors out of the market? Beyond that lie the questions of money supply amounts and the questions regarding balanced government budgets and the

---

4. 1 Corinthians 6:1-8.

social issues of entitlements. For this present discussion we must limit ourselves to the issues of taxation policies and appropriate regulations.

SUGGESTED POLICIES FOR CREATING MORE CAPITAL AND JOBS

"Render to all what is due them: tax to whom tax is due..."
Romans 13:7

As I have stated throughout this book, from the Christian perspective, scriptural principles should be the point of departure for any discussion regarding personal or social ethics, behavior, or organizational social systems. This sometimes presents significant challenges regarding the social system's applications for several reasons: 1) ancient Israel was a theocracy and prior to Christ's return we have no such expectation, 2) Israel was politically decentralized beyond any modern nation state and "primitive" relative to its methods of agrarian production with virtually no technological division of labor processes. Therefore, any direct extrapolations present a measure of challenges. Finding the core principles and having the wisdom to see their current applications strategically and with discernment as to their incremental application is the challenge of our assignment.

Taxation policy presents one such challenge; the essential changes we must make are obvious while overhauling the whole system will definitely require incremental changes. For the sake of historical context, prior to proposing modern applications, here are the most significant points to be made:

- Israel had no "secular" taxes per se, save the poll tax which was minimal. As a theocracy the primary tithe taxes were administered and spent through the ecclesiastic jurisdiction of the culture.

- Israel had no consumption- based taxes. Consumption-based taxes are highly "regressive"; that is, they take a much greater percentage of income from middle and lower income citizens than they do from the wealthy. Modern cultures are filled with regressive sales taxes and therefore constantly are requiring the less able to pay a higher proportion of their resources.

- Israel's taxation system, except for the poll tax, was paid in agricultural products rather than currency.

- The tithe taxation system was a "flat tax." It was uniform for all levels of wealth and applied to all forms of increase. It was set at a level of slightly over 20 percent. It was used to support the educational functions of society through the Levitical system and the support of priests dealing with the issues of spiritual values on behalf of both individuals and the entire community. A tithe for the poor was collected every three years. Along with gleaning it was used to provide for the poor and administered locally.

- The "producers" (agriculturally) were required to only harvest their crops on a "one cut" basis, leaving the corners of their fields and any second harvest remainders for the financially less able to glean and harvest freely. Obviously, this concept of gleaning as a means of support for the less able is being widely used in the western Christian-based world and has helped support significant numbers of citizens over the centuries in terms of food distribution excess or slightly damaged goods and other creative opportunities for the poor to be able to have the dignity of participating in their own provision.

- All forms of wealth transfer using modern parlance were designed to enhance the possibility of self-reliance and productivity for all citizens while reinforcing the common social culture of compassion and mutual responsibility for the welfare of the entire community.

Having briefly noted these things, here are some specific recommendations I offer to stimulate global discussions regarding taxation reform where applicable:

1. Here in the United States the current taxation system is an absurdly confused and truncated patchwork of duplicated regulations and obtuse reasoning which promotes evasion, "insider" privilege, and a general disrespect for the surrounding social systems. Rigorously simplifying it based on some of the following concepts

is of the highest priority and appropriate to do as an essential part of getting out of our current confusion.

2. Determining which level of government—local, regional or national—is primarily responsible for proposed services and therefore has the right to tax to fund them must be clearly determined before any taxation policy is established.

3. Determining which jurisdiction of social government is responsible for taxation whether the individual family, church, or business is equally compelling before tax policies are set.

4. Property taxation has no biblical precedence since, "The earth is the LORD's" (Psalm 24:1) and taxing land is viewed as attempting to tax God. Property-related fees for protection such as police and fire, etc., and for social responsibilities such as building codes, sanitation, etc., and the like are clearly appropriate. Property taxes' linkage to education is viewed by numbers of believers as a principal reason that public education is deteriorating. We all know that an educated citizenry is essential to both freedom and sustainable prosperity. A general voucher system would restore both choice and efficiency through performance to the nation's citizens.

5. All increase whether personal or corporate should be taxed. This will immediately create a more equitable system.

6. The sum total of all income taxes for the various taxation jurisdictions should be in the general range of 20 percent. Some exemptions should be considered such as the poverty line, charity, and employment incentives for hiring.

7. As noted, consumption taxes are regressive and should be phased out.

8. All inheritance taxes should be eliminated. Generational momentum should be encouraged as well as private charity as the cornerstone of social care that is relationally-based rather than impersonally and institutionally-based.

9. The concept of a "living wage", once a foundational concept in the U.S. job market, should be established as a benchmark for employers to seek to meet, especially for those caring for families. Until the private sector actively seeks to care for those in genuine need, the government will continue to do so at the same levels of inefficiency, duplication, and institutional impersonality. When we as citizens love our neighbors as ourselves, the government will have far, far less call upon our resources.

A BRIEF LOOK AT A BROKEN TAXATION SYSTEM

"If you believe that the system works and that hard work is rewarded, you will favor low taxes and low levels of redistribution. If, in contrast, you believe that the system is broken and corrupt, and that only insiders and cronies are rewarded, you will favor high taxes and high levels of redistribution."

Reihan Salam, "Beyond Tax Cuts,"
National Review, December 1, 2008, p. 32

As many of you know, only about half of the people in the United States pay any federal income tax. That of course means that half of our citizens are not paying any income tax. Both groups are paying the taxes on gasoline, sales tax, and other "hidden taxes" directly or indirectly. Nevertheless, as a nation we must ask ourselves: What does it mean when our nation's federal expenditures are largely being financed by only half the people? Is that fair? Another way to look at this issue is to go the other direction and ask: Does this mean that the economic system is only working well enough that half the citizens' income is so low that they are exempt from federal taxes? There are people whose income is very high and they have found their way around the system's tax loopholes or deductions, but certainly, only a small percentage of these excluded masses pay no federal income taxes. Nevertheless, both of the above questions raise some serious discussions depending on which way one looks at this issue. Whatever else it does say, it says that the citizens gaining the most general benefit from the economic system are in fact paying the federal government's bills almost exclusively by themselves.

Having taken note of these two different perspectives, let us now briefly look at an article written in 2008 that speaks directly to where our taxation system stands:

> "If the tax forms you're filing this year show Uncle Sam entitled to any income tax, you increasingly stand alone. The income tax system is so bad, and increasingly reliant on a shrinking number of Americans to pay the nation's bills, that 40% of the country's households—more than 44 million adults—pay no income taxes at all. Not a penny.

> "Think of it this way. After dropping off your tax forms at the Post Office, you find 100 people standing on the sidewalk. Forty of them will be excused from paying income taxes thanks to Congress. Twenty of them, the middle class, will pay barely a thing. The forty who remain, the upper middle class and the wealthy, will pay nearly all of the income taxes.

> "Look at that crowd again and find the richest person there. That individual will pay 37% of all the income taxes owed by those 100 people. The 10 richest people in the crowd will pay 71% of the income-tax bill. The 40 most successful people will pay 99% of everyone's income taxes. Yet for some lawmakers in Washington, these taxpayers aren't paying enough. Our tax system comes up short in a lot of areas. It doesn't foster economic growth. It isn't very simple. And it certainly isn't fair. The one place where it does excel is at redistributing income."

> Ari Fleisher, "The Taxpaying Minority,"
> *The Wall Street Journal*, April 16, 2007, p. A15

Fleisher's article goes on at some length to show how a smaller and smaller group of people are paying a higher and higher percentage of our nation's tax bills, and this trend is rising every year. Once again, there are different ways to look at this but for now I will say that a larger and larger group of Americans is paying no income taxes, while at the same time our national deficit is growing by trillions every year, which tells us especially that at some time those who are funding this debacle will revolt. It also tells me that our wage rates in numbers of areas need to rise, our taxation rates need to drop, our deficits need to cease, and, because this will make numbers of American-made goods and services globally more expensive and therefore less globally competitive, we need to significantly increase our "buy local and buy American" efforts.

Hard choices are upon us in many areas. Nations, like individuals, are going to have to decide in multiple areas how they will support a paid-for lifestyle and some of the challenging trade-offs that will go with these choices. Now we are back to the title of this book *On the Destiny of Nations,* and the nations' need to make the choices and chart the course of who they want to be in the future as the result of the challenging choices now facing us all. We are also back to the issue of the consequence of the new leaders committed to help us resolve these issues. Those new leaders will be the ones helping the citizens define their choices, accept the consequences of those choices, and move into Phase Three of this great global economic reset. Whatever that will all look like, we Christians cannot and must not attempt to approach these choices based primarily on our political orientations; those orientations will be insufficient. We must approach these times from a Kingdom perspective; humbly, in the fear of God and love for people, and recognizing that ultimately these choices are not about lifestyle. They are about who we are as representatives of Christ to His nations and how we can help them see Him in us. These choices are bridges into the kinds of eternal choices one makes in light of eternity.

CAPITAL FORMATION, EMPLOYMENT, AND ECONOMIC HOPE

As we know, capitalism must be protected from a number of its own negative possibilities which are driven, not so much by the system itself, but rather by the fallen natures of people utilizing the system for personal advantage with little heart or consideration for the others in the system. Capitalism can be driven either by love or social

Darwinism. All economic systems represent the values driving the systems. Marriages fail but Jesus came to redeem the institution of marriage. So it is with economic systems; the closer they conform to biblical values, the more redeemable they are. What makes capitalism so powerful is the choice-driven hope behind it, the power to dream and imagine, and put one's life behind those dreams. "All in" so to speak, behind those dreams. I personally know something about those dreams and what they cost to make them happen, having started a business from scratch and slept on the office floor to give it the fullest attention to succeed. That is capitalism; hope that grows into a tangible enterprise, collecting people as it grows and growing with them. Some of you know exactly what I am saying. You have been there, too.

Capital is hope and vision that came to pass. If the government or any other obstacle becomes seemingly so large that it quenches the dream, or quenches enough dreams of enough people, the whole system slows to a crawl. The last entity that can reignite it is the government unless it convinces enough dreamers that it really does want to create a climate that is dream-friendly and therefore job-creating friendly. Dreams employ people if they are fed. Capitalism, from the entrepreneurial side, involves dreams and sacrifice in motion. I would remind us once again, most of the harshest criticisms of capitalism are properly directed towards the giants of the system where power and impersonal ethics tend to feed short-term greed and practices that in no way reflect the 80 percent of capital producers and the millions of people who work with and for them.

WHY THE MIDDLE CLASS IS SO IMPORTANT

"Upward mobility from the bottom is
the crux of the American promise."

Mitch Daniels, Governor of Indiana

Most economists agree on the central importance of the need for an expanding middle class within any healthy economy. The middle class is the unspoken target of most people's aspirations as they see the opportunity to improve their lifestyle. Some may aspire to be moguls of the media or titans of business, but the largest number of people by far simply wants a more comfortable lifestyle and more discretionary time to enjoy life and relationships. Therefore, it is of real concern that recent studies seem to indicate that here in the U.S. our middle class is falling backward relative to economic positions within the economy. I strongly suspect this is true in most of the so-called advanced economies of the world as the causes and effects of this economic crisis persist. This situation will not be easily or quickly fixed. Too many other foundational economic issues must be addressed, not the least of which is to stop the bleeding of debt creation in the national budgets of multiple nations and resolve how these gigantic debts are going to be paid.

More government spending, which is the remedy of the Keynesian economists we discussed, will surely not resolve the problem. As Einstein wisely observed, the level of thinking that created a problem is insufficient to resolve it. More government stimulus spending will only signal to an increasing number of people who see the futility of this approach that government leaders still don't get it, and therefore those who advocate such approaches will only continue to create more problems for taxpayers and the business community as well. The core issues, once having begun to be resolved, will be evidenced by a sustainable increase in consumer consumption, while at the same time a reduction in their levels of personal debt. Undergirding this will be major simplifications of the tax codes, the gradual introduction of asset-backed currencies, and increased employment. More of this discussion is coming in the next chapter. As we have noted before, until faith is restored in the people, especially business leaders, the system will remain on life-support levels.

Using the rhetoric of class warfare for political gain is suicidal for a nation and those who seek to govern it. What made America so successful was not its focus on eliminating classes, but rather its focus on character as the means by which one's life could be economically rewarded. Character in this context is spelled "hard work, savings, and sacrifice for others." All of those letters spell "success" if enough people in the system believe in those values and practice them, and we are back to values once again. All successful economic roads lead to the common hub of values that align with our common Creator.

GENERAL CONCLUSIONS REGARDING CAPITAL

Capital creation has a number of components and stimulants as we just discussed in a general way. All of those components are based on aligning ourselves and our systems with what God says is important to Him, which is that our lives begin to allow us to live and experience the realities and joys of life itself, as He Himself is experiencing them. God saved us to bring us into His life.[5]

That journey requires clarity on the distinctive differences between material and economic blessings if you will, which God wants to share with all mankind, and the capacity to draw real Kingdom life from them because you are spiritually healthy enough to do so. Spiritual health is essential to truly enjoy material blessings. Therefore, I want to close this chapter with some brief but essential comments on the value of upward material mobility within any culture by understanding the differences between wealth and riches.

The distinction between wealth and riches is critical to the ongoing formation of economic prosperity within the family unit and generational strategic empowerment. Simply stated, "riches" are perishable assets, which Christ warned us not to focus improperly on as the primary goal of our labors.[6] Riches can be initially gained with or without ethics and morals. "Wealth" on the other hand, is primarily achieved through the skills, spiritual knowledge, and character developed in obeying God's ways of approaching resource management. Riches are something we have; wealth is something we are. Our job is to put our hearts into what is a treasure to God, which is the wealth He has for us in Christ. Then we properly let the riches that God chooses to give us take their appointed course in our lives according to our calling. Wealth will pass

---

5. Romans 5:10; John 14:6.
6. Matthew 6:20.

through death, but riches will not.[7] There are five biblically definable elements of wealth:

1. Relational peace with God

2. Relationships God has given you

3. Revelational wealth

4. Time

5. Material contentment

All these attributes of wealth are to be studied carefully and transmitted from parents to children and generation to generation. It is the work of family units to build wealth across the generations. We have noted these things earlier, but I would remind us of them again; there is no substitute for generational momentum and the knowledge and character to generate economic prosperity for the greatest number of people.

Bless God for the ability to turn dreams into capital and employ others at wages that pass on that blessing. Bless God for leaders and governments that truly understand how to create an atmosphere where free men and women can live in an economic system of free and honest exchanges using honest currencies to do so. Bless God for cultures that understand that the insertion of spiritual values into every part of that culture is essential for its survival and ability to add true value to the people. And, bless God for the ability to see the value of material blessings, but recognize that it is spiritual wealth that puts the flavor of life into them, transforming them into food for the soul, inspiration to the spirit, and health and blessing to the body.

> "'We are in a world that has a system that now allows the convergence among many billions of people, and we had better step back and figure out what it means. It would be a nice coincidence if all the things that were true before

---

7. Matthew 6:19-20; 1 Corinthians 3:9-15.

are still true now—but there are quite a few things you actually need to do differently...You need to have a much more thoughtful national discussion.'"

Dinakar Singh, in Thomas L. Friedman's *The World Is Flat*, 2005, p. 375

CHAPTER 8

ON THE INSTRUMENTS OF EXCHANGE:
TRUST, LIMITS, AND MONEY

In this chapter, specifically dealing with economics policy, we will discuss how the trust of the system is directly and indirectly affected by agreed upon limits and restraints exercised within the system by those most responsible for its control. Economic systems run on people's trust. We will also be dealing with the true value of the currencies of exchange within the system. Trust asks: Is the game fair or rigged? Are the people running it competent to do so? How do we fix it if it needs fixing?? Economics can become complex but ultimately questions of trust and fairness become basic issues.

Economics requires instruments of exchange. In an economic transaction a product or service is exchanged for another product or service of similar value (bartering), or both are converted to some form of currency that represents common value to both parties and that currency is then exchanged. Economics is about agreed upon value for any object or service of exchange and then deciding the form of payment that will be used to expedite the transaction. The currency, or commonly the "money" must have an agreed upon value, and in the modern world, must have a common currency that all other currencies are converted into (the U.S. dollar). Undergirding all this is the trust among all the parties using the system.

ENGAGING PEOPLE AND SYSTEMS BEYOND NECESSITY

Any economy can exist and function based on people engaging one another out of the sheer necessity for food, shelter, clothing, and other basic needs. However, such an economy will never move beyond that primitive level until the common element of trust pervades the system. Growing economies run on participants' trust and when that trust is withdrawn by sufficient numbers of people—especially by those managing and supplying the largest amounts of capital—that system will stall, recede, and eventually collapse if trust is not restored. I have just described where we now are on the most basic of levels; trust has been significantly withdrawn within our global economy. However much it may appear to have been restored, until the fundamental issues we are addressing have been resolved, patches of trust and glimmers of hope will be transitory and even dangerous. As the Scripture says, "Hope deferred makes the heart sick",[1] but hope extended and then dashed endangers things altogether.

Capitalism is particularly vulnerable to the necessity of hope by its participants. Private citizens are investing in the system by deferring current consumption and investing their savings into future ventures, or even going into debt to acquire things based on their presumptions of future employment and stable currencies. In a more socialistic system, the government is the primary investor and hope is not the government's primary concern; a socialist government's concern involves control over the citizens and how they respond to the choices made by their rulers. Capitalistic systems run on trust and authoritarian systems run on control. In capitalism, people must trust in the people managing the private sector, the politicians overseeing them, and their abilities to maintain economic stability, national and domestic order, and the wisdom to adequately respond quickly to abnormalities and breakdowns anywhere within those systems.

THE ECONOMIC NECESSITY OF TRUSTING LEADERS

Let us now discuss four major elements of trust which are required to keep an economy growing and expanding rather than simply reverting

---

1. Proverbs 13:12.

back to the minimal necessities of sustainable exchanges characterizing a flat economy.

1. The Issue of Character: Character trumps virtually all other qualifiers for trust in a leader. Even if a leader is technically qualified for a position, if they do not have character, then their placement in any position of responsibility is problematic. Character assumes the virtues of honesty, integrity, discipline, team play, selflessness, love, and other critical attributes.[2] If those leading the system are not perceived as having these traits, then the nature or effectiveness of the economic system itself is a secondary issue. The management of the system is commonly viewed as more important than the system itself. So how do we establish these spiritual virtues in the culture? We must inject Christ's message of meaningful community and shared values in every strategic way possible into the fabric of the nation.

   We are back to where we have already been numbers of times; Christians must engage the system, and not just on the grounds of where we object or find fault with the current culture or legislation. We must become a positive force in our cultures rather than just the resident critic. "Values clarification" currently has to do primarily with the agenda of so-called "diversity." We need a whole different kind of values clarification than simply sexual orientation or "tolerance." We need a spiritual renaissance to permeate all our political and economic leaders and thus our systems. Properly applied, tolerance is a meaningful value, but it has little to do with economic growth.

2. The Issue of Expertise: There is a difference between desire and ability. One may have all the will and desire in the world to accomplish something or hold some position but still not have the skill sets or competencies to do so. This is a major issue relative to the election to public office of many of our past and current office holders, or important management positions within our system by those appointed by office holders. It should be abundantly clear by now that we have many officials on all levels of government

---

2. Galatians 5:22-23.

who do not have an adequate grasp of economic principles to be in positions where they are making budget and expenditure decisions. Many of them also lack the expertise to understand the consequences of those decisions. Having greatly "dumbed down" our educational systems, it is almost impossible for the electorate to adequately vet or exercise due diligence relative to a candidate's qualifications for public office since the electorate does not have the knowledge to recognize those qualified for office. This current crisis is bringing this reality front and center. The adequate education of the citizenry is a prerequisite for the competency of those governing them.

How can we have faith in our leaders if we do not have an adequate knowledge of the principles by which to judge their competencies? I believe that significant numbers of the general public are becoming increasingly aware of their own inadequacies in terms of sufficient knowledge of economic principles to elect wise leaders. This is making them all the more uncertain as to how their nations will be able to recover and be set on the proper course to avoid these challenges in the future.

3. The Issue of Relational Influences and Connections: People are heavily influenced by their friends and colleagues and one of the best ways to know who somebody really is, and what they truly believe, is to know about a person's key relationships.[3] People deserve to know who is influencing their leaders. Trust is built on a clear confidence about who the "real person" actually is behind the public posturing or the persona that goes with a particular office or responsibility. Trust in a public official is also difficult if we do not know how that potential office holder views the borders, limits, and responsibilities of the office they would hold before they take the actual position. I have personally seen more than one situation where office holders responded very differently once in office than we were led to believe about them when they ran as candidates. We are back once more to trust based on accurate expectations and honest disclosure.

3.   1 Corinthians 15:33.

4. The Issue of Personal Investments and Conflicts of Interest: We extend trust in people or systems when we are clear that the people managing the system, and the system itself, is not subject to easy manipulation for personal advantage, and operates with sufficient oversight to prohibit such misuse. Trust presupposes that those representing us or managing the system for us are honoring all those who gave them the trust to do so fairly and with integrity. While many public offices require not only disclosure of possible conflicts of interest, and the divesting of potential conflicts, if their hearts are not pure in this regard they will find ways around the spirit of those rules while still possibly honoring the letter of the law. When this happens, or happens frequently, trust in the system will "freeze" until sufficient correction appears. Trust in the giants of the financial investment sectors currently reflects little trust by the general public. Too many examples of conflicted interests have come forth.

All of the above four points are offered as simple and basic explanations for much of what has happened to accentuate and extend this current economic crisis. People have lost confidence in both the managers and overseers of the system and even in the system itself to varying degrees. To talk about "recovery" is naïve at best and dangerous at worst. Not only have elements of the system proven their brokenness, many of the most fundamental issues of the breakdown have not been addressed, including: the proper balance of private sector choice and government planning in the roll of modern economics and government; the desirability of generational financial momentum for family units, and the values and economic environment required to stimulate prudent personal spending; the political climate required to stimulate capital creation in an economy, and the taxation policies and other supplemental programs needed to produce maximum employment as a result of those stimulants; and the issues of trust, regulations, and currency-banking policies which we will further discuss in this chapter. Let us now continue to examine the necessity of limits and boundaries from other necessary perspectives as they affect trust and investment in the realm of economic systems.

LIMITS ON POWER: THE EFFECT OF SAFETY

"'From any tree of the garden you may eat freely; but from the tree of the knowledge of good and evil you shall not eat, for in the day that you eat from it you will surely die.'"

Genesis 2:16-17

Since the Garden of Eden, mankind has been dealing with the issue of limits. Adam and Eve believed Satan's lie that God had established limits on their freedom out of fear for His own position of power and authority. Nothing could have been further from the truth as Christ's death on the Cross proved: Jesus died to share power, freedom, and life with man, and deliver him from an eternal state of weakness and sin. While we do live in a world where limits are certainly used by some to protect themselves and ensnare and weaken others, limits and boundaries are an inherent gift from God to keep us safe from many different kinds of harm and even death. Like any loving parent, God is constantly using limits to keep man from prematurely touching and experiencing things that would greatly harm us until we are mature enough to be guided by God to do so. Many limits are essential and safeguard those who observe them while bringing great harm and death to those who don't.

Gravity is a limit the value of which you soon discover if you are falling toward the earth from any appreciable height. Fire creates limits as do water and air. Burning buildings, raging floods and tornados prove my point; observing precautionary limits keeps us from them or helps us survive them. Telling the truth is protection from the consequences of telling lies, as is faithfulness from the challenges of adultery or moral failure of any kind. Limits are found in both the material world and the spiritual world. Again, responsible parenting teaches children at an early age to respect limits if they want to avoid pain and trouble. Rebels break rules and limits; the consequences vary in both severity and the time it takes to manifest the consequences.

Some rules and limits are of human origin and are foolish, prejudicial, and should be eliminated. However, the limits God has established are not really broken by man; they break man when he breaks them. As we will shortly see, there are also serious economic limits and boundaries which carry serious consequences. We are in the beginning stages of suffering some of those consequences for breaking them now.

LIMITS AND THE CONSEQUENCES OF CORRUPTION

Adam and Eve eventually suffered the consequences of mortality and death when they bypassed God's limits. In the short run, they were morally corrupted by the sin nature and bondage to Satan that immediately followed their disobedience. Ask the alcoholic and heroin addict if the "freedom" to misuse drugs can ensnare and affect one's character; both their addiction and their words will confirm it. Obedience keeps us safe and once broken, it is often very hard to free oneself from the "open door" that was created in the process of disobedience. Godly morality is not a burden; it is a barrier and a bulwark against the loss of one's will to resist that which ensnares and addicts us. As the apostle Paul labors to convince us in chapter seven of the book of Romans, the Law reveals how corrupt our nature became in the Fall. Sin is not simply breaking a law; it is an inherent power contaminating our soul, eating away at our character, and constantly urging us to break free of the limits God has set for us. The Law reveals the depth of our corruption rather than being a limitation of our freedom.

Laws and principles are totally indifferent to our intentions. Even if we break them with good intentions, the consequences frequently corrupt us with bitterness and anger since we suffer without "deserving it" as we seek to justify our ignorance or good motives. We are thereby exposed to new and deeper opportunities to break more laws and principles, further adding to the loss of our freedom. One bypassed limit opens up multiple new limits to break, further enslaving us or the systems we create in our foolishness.

POWER IS GUARDED BY PROBLEMS

"Only rebel not ye against the LORD, neither fear ye the people of the land; for they are bread for us: their defence is departed from them, and the LORD is with us: fear them not."

Numbers 14:9, KJV

Caleb and Joshua clearly understood that our problems, obstacles, or perceived enemies can in fact become "food" for us if we see them as opportunities to think or act differently and use them to take us to new levels of understanding and competencies. New levels of personal power or new levels of enhanced performance are often "guarded" by the barriers of current problems we have not yet mastered. Problems hold us at the current levels of our competencies until we break free of those levels and replace them with new insights and new behaviors. Problem solving is an exercise in enhanced freedoms.

Problems are also often a gift in disguise; they protect us from levels of responsibility or power that would or could harm or destroy us if we were to receive them at our current levels of knowledge or maturity. In eternity it is clear that we will have levels of knowledge and power beyond where we now are in this present life. In fact, life on earth is where our character is formed and strengthened so as to be able to handle new levels of spiritual responsibility in eternity.

As humans we are given more and more responsibility here on earth based on our abilities to respond to them. None of us want to be "set up to fail" so to speak, even in this life by being promoted beyond our capacities. Problems often serve not only as signals of complications beyond our capacities to solve them; they serve as barriers to our possible destruction. Those who do not understand this reality, and insist on rushing ahead of their unsolved problems, often cause great harm to both themselves and others who follow their lead. Breaking barriers to new levels of achievement is one thing; ignoring our own current limitations or someone else's limitations is quite another. Recklessness is no more a virtue than ignorance. Leaders and those who run systems must understand and practice the self-restraint of knowing their own limits or the limitations of those who follow them.

LIMITS, GREED, AND IGNORANCE

We are here today because numbers of our nations' leaders and their economic and financial advisors, were either ignorant of principles that leaders in their positions cannot afford to be ignorant of, or because greed or some other debilitating character flaw overcame them. The core issue here is that selfish gain and ambition can and do cloud one's vision and drive them to bypass limits,[4] known or unknown, dragging those following them into the consequences of their stupidity.

How important is it that the men and women who lead and influence both the private and public sectors of our cultures and nations are people of proven character? It is obviously critically important. They must have sufficient character, and safeguards within the systems themselves, to protect the people from the great harm that befalls them when corruption overcomes their leaders. How then do we maximize the possibility of their leaders having sufficient character for their jobs, and how does the general citizenry have sufficient character to discern character, or the lack thereof, when they see it? That answer is equally obvious. We must inject godly values into the culture and nation everywhere and continuously. How, who, and where is that to come from? The answer is equally obvious and compelling; it is the church, her leaders, and her people. We must make the "welfare of the city" our welfare, too, and not just our own welfare or the condition of our own churches or families.[5] To become a truly healthy people, and a truly healthy spiritual community, our love and concern must model loving our neighbors and their welfare. Love requires the handiwork of educating ourselves for the overall good of the communities in which we live. Love educates to protect, provide, and promote the welfare of people.

How can we tell if we are doing this? Jesus said, "Where your treasure is, there your heart will be."[6] Our treasure generally consists of three things: our time, our talents, and our financial resources. How are our church leaders encouraging us to spend those three resources? I have no doubt that the local church community must care for and empower its own needs. Nevertheless, our church budgets are a prime indicator of how we feel about loving our neighbors. How are we doing in that regard, especially in terms of training our people to influence and educate others with godly values and knowledge both personally and

---

4. Luke 12:15.
5. Jeremiah 29:7.
6. Matthew 6:21.

socially as we model them ourselves? Our current national cultures give us a very accurate picture of how we are doing. Our treasure has certainly not served our neighbors very well. Their moral and spiritual decline is clearly reflected in the economic defunding of our societies.

In summary, people trust other people or systems that have proven their character, values, competencies, and commitments to create and maintain justice and others' well-being.

We will now examine some specific economic and financial policies which either are, or should be, under serious scrutiny as to their inherent worthiness to warrant our trust. While our citizens may be relatively ignorant of the principles of a choice-based economy, the essential benefits of generational financial momentum, and the relationship between capital formation, taxation, and employment levels, they seem to intuitively withhold trust from leaders or practices that ignore the limitations and boundaries of financial spending. That is likely the case because they are aware, on a regular basis, of having to function within financial limits and boundaries themselves, and the penalties of not doing so. After all, economics is about household management.

CURRENCY, FIAT MONEY, AND BANKING

In the years between the early 1960s and the early 1970s, a series of destructive spiritual forces were unleashed upon the world, especially in the United States. Prayer in school was banned, no-fault divorce was inaugurated, abortion was legalized, and the gold standard backing currencies was abandoned. In turn, we have experienced the massive deterioration and secularization of public education, the end of traditional families for millions, the wholesale slaughter of the unborn, and the detachment of restraints on the printing of money throughout the world.

As we have discussed, all of these things helped bring us to this present crisis; each one has had massive impact on the world's economies. The voters became increasingly incapable of electing wise leaders, generational economic momentum was vastly reduced for the middle class, and the demographics of abortion made most social entitlements untenable. Each one of these social decrees emboldened the secular forces as they continued in their crusade to drive Judeo-Christian values out of the public square. Now, in this chapter, we must address the consequences of fiat money; that is, currencies disconnected from real substances backing up their value.

THE "LIMITLESS" PHENOMENA OF FIAT MONEY

"You shall do no wrong in judgment, in measurement of weight or capacity. You shall have just balances, just weights, a just ephah, and a just hin; I am the LORD your God, who brought you out from the land of Egypt."

Leviticus 19:35-36

"Fiat money has no place to go, but to gold."

Alan Greenspan, Former chairman, the Federal Reserve Board,
Council on Foreign Relations speech, September 15, 2010

"Just weights and measures" means honest money; that is, a currency that has the actual trading value that it says it has. Modern currency is indeed traded for its "stated value," but that value is backed only by the promise that the one who issued it gives to its holder, rather than the actual value of the currency itself. The currency itself is virtually worthless. There is nothing of tangible value behind it but a promise. It is paper representing words, not commodities of any kind. So far, those promises have been honored and I have no doubt about the future intentions of governmental issuers of the world's currencies to continue to do so.

The issue is not their desire to do so but rather their ability. Our current crisis is challenging that ability to fulfill their promises on two counts: the economic viability of the systems behind these governments is weakening, and secondly, the trading value of their currencies will have been radically diluted due to the inflation caused by the amounts of new money they will continue to need to print in an attempt to pay off their nation's massive debts.

As you know, when the nations went off the gold standard backing their currencies in 1972, the currencies became fiat money' that is, money having no intrinsic value beyond the promises of governments to pay the face amounts of their financial instruments. This means that new money can be created "out of thin air" in order to meet financial needs. It is neither backed by nor limited to the amount of any tangible substance of value giving it tradable worth. Of course, the economists of each nation keep track of the money supply in order to see the levels of dilution taking place as new money is created. But since the game is about trust, not actual value, a currency's inflation is simply factored into the exchange rates between competing currencies. Inflation is an assumed part of the game but is to be minimized as much as possible by the management of each nation's leaders. Fiat money makes the management of inflation by cost-of-living increases very, very important because it not only affects the cost of living internally within a particular nation, it affects both their ability to secure government loans and their balance of trade between other nations based on the increased costs of their products. The Scriptures address inflation due to currencies' dilution by lesser substances as a serious sin on a number of occasions.[7] Please remember this: a mere 1.5 percent annual increased cost of living increase, due to inflated currency adjustments, is a 15 percent increase every decade. This is a staggering reality for people living on fixed incomes and makes savings or good stewardship an exercise in futility.

As we raise again the specter of massive government debt affecting multiple nations, and growing by the day, the necessity of increasing the money supplies, and hence diluting their values, becomes greater every day. Since all the major players are very aware of all this, and the insecurities of the market are so great, the banks hold on to depositors' money and make loans harder and harder to acquire. They neither want to increase the possibility of further bad loans, nor risk insolvency by having insufficient currencies to pay off the bad loans they have yet to declare or negotiate. During our recent government bailouts, the majority of the banks' government-loaned money here in the United States, once it stabilized the banks, has remained there for the sake of the banks' own financial risks rather than being used to stimulate business investments as was intended by the government.

---

7.   Proverbs 20:10, 23; 25:4; Isaiah 1:22, 25.

FRACTIONAL RESERVE BANKING:
ACTUARIAL GENIUS OR INFLATIONARY DEMON?

"Your silver has become dross, Your wine mixed with water."

Isaiah 1:22, NKJV

The fractional reserve banking system, wherein deposits into the banks are loaned out at multiple times the amounts of the actual deposits themselves, adds to the increase in the money supplies. Banks are only required to hold minimal amounts of actual deposited funds so as to permit the "leveraging" of money available to them to make more loans and invest those funds into profitable investments for the banks. The "spread" they make between the interest they receive on their loans and what they pay to the actual depositors of the money is therefore multiplied up to as many times as they re-loaned or invested that money as it proliferated through the system. Bank reserve requirements, based on both actuarial estimates of investor withdrawals at any given time and the government's promise to insure investors' money and limit their withdrawals if necessary, vary for different kinds of accounts but a 10 percent reserve requirement allows a $100 deposit to produce $500 of loans once it has moved through the banking system. It is "magic," but God is not in favor of magic, especially when someone is using your money to make magic for themselves and giving you a small portion of what your money actually produced for them. The even more minuscule amounts paid in 2012 on bank deposit accounts reflects the fact that banks are not loaning the money they typically do.

As many of you know, the Scriptures require asset-backed money, seven-year maximum term loans, non-interest bearing loans to the poor, and a fifty-year jubilee designed to reorder the system.[8] While all of those principles would have to be adapted to a non-agrarian-based economy, and that economy would have to accept Judeo-Christian values to do so, for us as believers the Scriptures' principles should be our point of departure for any evaluation of their modern economic adaptations to their respective elements of society.

---

8.   Deuteronomy 15:1; Leviticus 25:8-55.

What is clear to me is that our banking systems need to be overhauled and repositioned. They should be primarily secure places for the storage of our assets, and not further diluting our money through the fractional reserve system. I have no problem with investment banking but the value given to the depositors should be related equitably with those particular types of banks. The older models of the merchant banks, wherein the banks helped people succeed in their venture loans, rather than living off the interests of loans with guaranteed secured assets from the loanees, were more biblical. These merchant banks were much more aligned with a spirit of cooperation rather than a spirit of opportunism.

WHAT I BELIEVE IS COMING

By the time we get to Phase Three of the crisis through the turmoil, breakdowns, and reordering of the systems in Phase Two, I expect to see some of the following major changes in the financial world. However, if Phase Two gets to price controls and massive debt defaults, which it may well, these new regulations may well become even steeper and more radical than I foresee.

While it is unrealistic to expect us to move quickly to fully asset-backed currency, I predict that this financial crisis will move toward partially-backed currencies with time schedules of both compliance and higher future levels of asset to currency percentages. I also believe that the reserve requirements on all banks, especially those engaging in international financing, will increase dramatically from their current inflationary levels. I further believe that the Federal Reserve Bank will be required to make public their operations, and have new levels of government restrictions placed on them. The federal governments of most, if not all, Western nations will be required by trade and currency agreements to balance their budgets and once the loan re-payments are renegotiated, loan limits will be forced on them by the international financial community limiting their loans to a specific ceiling of their GNP levels. The derivatives markets will be greatly regulated relative to leverage levels, and joint private enterprise-government agencies will take a more proactive regulatory role in specific areas of higher risk financial activities. While all of these changes will require major changes in the way we view and handle both money and how nations spend it, the current crisis will require at least these levels of change.

REGULATION SHOULD FOLLOW THE MONEY

Before we leave this section regarding currency and regulation I must reemphasize a critical point once again. The challenges and most serious dangers to modern capitalism and the general welfare of the people take place where the greatest amount of finance has accumulated. Regulation is most needed in the areas of greatest temptation and that is in the financial sectors of the economy, which are handling the accumulated investment capital of the people and the layers of government themselves which now consume between 37 and 42 percent of the GDP[9]. Capitalism needs general regulations, but as little as is possible, on the production and services end of the system. It needs the greatest scrutiny where large amounts of money can make huge personal gains on moving those large amounts of money.

More to the point, regulation must greatly limit putting those large amounts of money at absurd risk in an attempt to significantly leverage those assets. This is exactly what happened by those managing the financial systems both governmentally and in the private sectors. Add to this situation the unbalanced budgets and we are where we are. The 80+ percent of small business enterprises making the great bulk of the nation's GDP is not where the principal issues of the systems lie. As the old saying goes, "follow the money," and let's guard it well.

The most difficult part of these transitions will initially be faced by the gradual, but ultimately severe, loss of public support for elected officials of government due to major budget constraints on every level. Math and compassion are on a collision course. We are now experiencing them in Phase One of the crisis and it is still relatively early in the

---

9.   Jackie Calmes, "Government's Share (National Desk)," *New York Times*, January 8, 2012, A16; "Explore the Data, 2011 Index of Economic Freedom," Heritage Foundation and The Wall Street Journal. http://www.heritage.org/index/explore?view=by-variables.

journey. As we will see in the next chapter, this is where the church must make the difference. True human needs will increasingly have to be met by the private sector, volunteerism, and the resurgence of the caring nuclear family.

MATERIALISM, CONSUMPTION, AND LIFESTYLE

All of the coming pressures will force us all to look at our lifestyles and how we can and should make appropriate changes. Our God is not opposed to great wealth or economic struggles; He is opposed to waste, unbelief, and ingratitude. Capitalism, under the pressures of Keynesian economic philosophy, forces levels of consumption on the system in order to raise sufficient annual growth levels to service the debt created by government borrowing due to its overextensions of activities. That pressure feeds our fallen needs to consume more than is either required, or often healthy, both physically and spiritually.

Once again, God is not opposed to feasting, lavish celebrations, and excellence in all forms of buildings and embellishments of His created earthly environment.[10] He has clearly proven that by His command-ments in the Old Testament to feast and celebrate at least three times a year as an entire nation. His Temple was lavishly constructed and furnished, as was Solomon's.[11] The issue is this: We must hear God for our own levels of consumption and material expenditures, and balance that with the needs of others, and God's general investments in the spreading of His Kingdom. Indeed, we are back to loving God and loving our neighbors in our lifestyles.

> "You cannot serve God and mammon."
> Matthew 6:24

Mammon, as many of you know, is not a concept or even a human propensity to worship luxury or money. Mammon is an Old Testament rebellious angelic deity who is very much alive and active today. His domain of human corruption exercises pressure on man to worship

---

10. Deuteronomy 14:24-26; 16:8-17.
11. Regarding Solomon's temple: 2 Chronicles, chapters 2—7.

material provisions as the source of his well-being rather than worshiping the Creator of that wealth and trusting in His loving provision for all forms of our human welfare. Just like the other angelic-demonic rulers that Paul identified in Ephesians 6:12, mammon is committed to defile and dominate mankind and oppress his life with the worship of things other than God. If "success" is measured by obedience to God, and not the amount of power or material things we accumulate, then the proper levels of consumption must likewise be measured by that same standard.

The supreme and daunting question that we must all face when given the ability and opportunity to financially prosper is this: How much is enough? That is the question that we must keep before God. There is no magic formula, nor one given in the Scriptures. What we do know is that love for our neighbor, and investments in those in need, is both mandated and honored by God in many biblical verses, and demonstrated by all biblical heroes and heroines of the faith. What is upon us, and ready to increase in the coming years, are the challenges and opportunities to discover new levels of compassion and community within our neighborhoods, churches, places of work, and nations. Pressure, especially financial pressure, stretches us out and forces us to look up.

SOME CONCLUDING REMARKS

The limits and regulations required to establish and maintain both justice and productivity in any economic system is directly proportional to the spiritual values and disciplines of that system's citizens. That is what secularism must begrudgingly come to terms with. Secularism does not have the power to sufficiently motivate man's inner spiritual resources of love or self-government. Hence, it cannot produce or maintain in the long run a healthy economy built on inner restraints and outward generosity. What we believers must accept is this God-given mandate and responsibility to continuously function as salt and light within our nations. This mandate includes, but exceeds, mere charity or good works. The Kingdom of God is a lifestyle, not a series of programs.

True and genuine love for others is more than a duty performed or discipline extended. What has crippled our witness to the world, even more than the public scandal of our divisiveness and internal competitiveness, is our overall lack of love and concern for the general well-being of our communities and our nations. Yes, we are looking forward to the consummation of the Kingdom and our eternal future, and should be. What we must therefore understand as a result of that focus is that now the future is in many ways already in our hearts if we can but find it. When we do, it will be manifested by an appropriate balance between concern for the redeemed community and those yet outside of it. A truly Kingdom perspective is "now, but not yet" and "us, but them as well."

We must now move on to our concluding chapter of this very general and incomplete look at some of the causes, principles, and outcomes of our current economic reset. Our final comments will center not so much on the economics or possible remedies to our financial crisis, as it will on our need to focus on our responsibilities as dual citizens. On the one hand we Christians are called to "look upward," and on the other hand to look "around us." In both cases we will see real people with multiple needs, multiple gifts, and multiple choices to make. And if we look closely enough and inclusively at all these people, we will find the Kingdom we seek within our hearts.

CHAPTER 9

ON THE DESTINY OF NATIONS:
PUBLIC POLICY, COMMUNITY DEVELOPMENT,
AND THE SPIRITUAL POWER OF THE ECCLESIA

"God be gracious to us and bless us,...That Your way may be
known on the earth, Your salvation among all nations."

Psalm 67:1-2

APPLYING THE THREEFOLD CORD

As we arrive at our closing chapter, we must embrace once again the
necessary privilege of serving God and the people of the earth by
sharing with them the principles of God's life, and the vision He carries
passionately for them as individuals and nations. Discipling the nations
is ultimately an act of love carried out in a very strategic fashion by
leaders and people who are internally compelled by the Holy Spirit
to do so. It is done on three interrelated levels: through impacting
public policy, creating strong local communities, and pushing back the
demonic strongholds which hinder man's abilities to act freely in God.
This current crisis will be used by God to press the nations into new
levels of need and openness to the truths of God and the message
of His Kingdom. It is therefore now up to His people, especially His
leaders, to prepare to strategically and effectively engage on all three
of these interrelated levels and begin to release God's plan for the
nations held for such a time as this.

APOSTOLIC MINISTRY IS ESSENTIAL TO DISCIPLING

"...we are currently witnessing the most radical change in the way of 'doing church' since the Protestant Reformation. It is 'apostolic' because the recognition of the gift and office of the apostle is the most radical of a whole list of changes from the old wineskin."

C. Peter Wagner, *Apostles Today*, 2012, p. 90

"Therefore it says, 'WHEN HE ASCENDED ON HIGH, HE LED CAPTIVE A HOST OF CAPTIVES, AND HE GAVE GIFTS TO MEN.' (Now this expression, 'He ascended,' what does it mean except that He also had descended into the lower parts of the earth? He who descended is Himself also He who ascended far above all the heavens, so that He might fill all things.) And He gave [gifts] some as apostles, and some as prophets, and some as evangelists, and some as pastors and teachers, for the equipping of the saints for the work of service, to the building up of the body of Christ; until we all attain to the unity of the faith, and of the knowledge of the Son of God, to a mature man, to the measure of the stature which belongs to the fullness of Christ."

Ephesians 4:8-13

Apostles, beyond the original Twelve who served Jesus before His crucifixion, have populated the church since Christ ascended and released them into the body of Christ—the church—to do what only their ministry allows them to accomplish. They are not apostles like the Twelve or given to the writing of Scripture, but their engiftedness is essential to leading the church into her destiny as a ruler under Christ of His earthly Kingdom. Apostolic ministries are strategic ministries given to the church to help confirm the historic foundational doctrines from the Scriptures, to help establish local churches and help their leadership function, to give oversight to the other ministries within the church, and to help lead all of these functions into the strategic Kingdom work of discipling the nations prior to Christ's return. Not all apostles will do all of these things but all true apostles who are in the process of being recognized today will help reposition the church, where necessary, into the church's serving work within the Kingdom context, rather than the church simply serving Herself. That means, the church will function as an evangelistic herald, serving and equipping her members in every dimension of their lives and ministries, into all mankind.

The nations cannot and will not be discipled until the apostolic ministries define the work of the church in the context of the church's position within society. The church does not exist for herself but to serve the King and His Kingdom. This process will entail a major spiritual "revolution" so to speak, and begin to change not only the goals and structures of many congregations, but also the very nature of the leadership of the church itself. This economic and social values crisis is not only going to entail the bringing forth of very different leaders in society, it is going to bring forth equally new kinds of leaders into the church. Remember in Matthew 13:29, Jesus told His disciples that they could not pull up the tares from within the wheat because of their common root structure. This is exactly why anything that greatly affects the world system greatly affects the church, and vice versa.

Both sets of leaderships from the world system and the church are going to be severely affected by this crisis. As I have said already, this crisis will reveal and identify the leaders who will take us through it and into the new structures that will emerge from it. This crisis is only secondarily about man's failing social systems; it is primarily about repositioning global leadership to connect them to a Kingdom consciousness prior to Christ's return. As God's purposes march through history, He uses man's choices and foibles to call forth new leaders whose leadership causes the tectonic plates in the spiritual world to shift and realign themselves with God's progressive revelation of His Kingdom as we all move closer to His return. The following Scripture speaks to that march through history and the shifting spiritual plates being used in our current situation to further unveil His victorious Kingdom:

> "See to it that you do not refuse Him who is speaking.
> For if those did not escape when they refused him who
> warned them on earth, much less will we escape who

turn away from Him who warns us from heaven. And His voice shook the earth then, but now He has promised, saying, 'YET ONCE MORE I SHALL SHAKE NOT ONLY THE EARTH, BUT ALSO THE HEAVEN.' This expression, 'Yet once more,' denotes the removing of those things which can be shaken, as of created things, so that those things which cannot be shaken may remain. Therefore, since we receive a kingdom which cannot be shaken, let us show gratitude, by which we may offer to God an acceptable service with reverence and awe; for our God is a consuming fire."

Hebrews 12:25-29

SYNERGISM OF APOSTOLIC LEADERSHIP AND OTHER KINGDOM MINISTRIES AND POLICY EXPERTS

"Unless the people of God stand up as one against the onslaught of division, we will never reach the desired level of maturity or be at a place of readiness for His return."

Norman Willis, *Unity with a Return*, 1994, p. 5

God has revealed Himself as a "team player" since He has incorporated man into the leadership of His created order through Jesus Christ. Paul makes much of this fact in Romans 8 when he speaks at length of all of creation awaiting the maturation of mankind in Christ as the ones who will free the entire created order to fulfill its destiny.[1] Indeed, the Trinity itself speaks of both the reality of God in community within Him,[2] and as a clearly defined and functioning division of labor within Him,[3] as the Father, Son, and Holy Spirit go about their specific responsibilities in God's designated plans. As His children, we, too must learn to function in mutual appreciation and need as each member of the body supplies its own God-endowed gifts to the process of our completion in Him. So it is in His Kingdom: all the functions of gifts and assignments must cooperate. Society is so complex that every member of the body of

---

1. Romans 8:17-23.
2. Genesis 1:26.
3. John 14:10, 16, 26, 31.

Christ must discover their placement and be trained and equipped to contribute their gifts to the challenges we will face in the rebuilding of whatever social changes take place as a result of this crisis. True leaders help everyone find their function and place and rejoice in our corporate achievements rather than focusing only on themselves or the other leaders. In the Kingdom of God there are no "little people."

As the apostles, prophets, evangelists, pastors, and teachers go about the equipping of the saints for their specific assignments in the Kingdom, and all jurisdictions of Kingdom work—in families, the marketplace-economic world, the church structures, and the multi-faceted dimensions of public policy and culture—teams of leaders and experts in their fields will find one another and be wonderfully bonded together to serve in local, national, and international endeavors on His behalf. Ministry teams will emerge in every dimension of culture over the coming decades as the excitement of the Kingdom realities become more and more commonly perceived and expressed. Part of the job of the leaders will also be to keep watch on the need for correct appraisals of where we are in both the coming processes of this current crisis, and also the times which follow our coming through it and out from it.

This three-phased crisis will not be over until the fundamental work God intends for it to do is done. Therefore, expect misleading reports of our coming out of the process that God is fermenting through this crisis prior to God's completed work. Many times, for example, people take the ups and downs of the stock market as a definitive indicator of the current state of the national or global economies. As a general rule, the stock markets are tactical reports about short-term trends or earning reports rather than dealing with the longer term strategic conditions of the economies of the world. It is critical for those who will be assuming significant positions of leadership both inside and outside of the church to be sufficiently connected with both seasoned prophetic ministries,[4] and experts in the fields of economics and social trends. When we throw into the mix the challenges of upcoming events in the Middle East, North Korea, terrorist activities, and the

---

4.   1 Corinthians 14:32.

turmoil that will come as the economic crisis goes deeper into Phase Two, it is clear that social confusion will prompt numerous misleading "words from God." The globally emerging leaders will be increasingly easy to identify. They will be consistently stable and will lead out of true concern for the people and the systems, making the necessary adjustments required that will bring about long-term stability to our social systems and their connections, and achieve the justice and righteousness that characterize Kingdom-based outcomes.

Now, we must more closely examine the majestic governing institution through which these multi-faceted ministries of Christ's Kingdom citizens will be used by God to serve the people of the earth. The executive branch of Christ's Kingdom must now mature more fully and take up her role as a truly functioning *ecclesia* (pronounced e-klay-SEE-ah).

> "So what is the church? The *Ecclesia* is Christ's governing body on the earth. We are responsible to heed His statutes, exercise 'vice-regency', and administrate His government. You can see this is a strange concept to the majority of churchgoers today. Yet, the Word of God is settled, and therefore Christ holds us accountable for the way we do it, or do not do it."
>
> Derek Prince, *As the Church Goes, So Goes a Nation,* compact disc

THE ECCLESIA: KEY HOLDER OF
THE KINGDOM AND DISCIPLER OF NATIONS

> "Now when Jesus came into the district of Caesarea Philippi, He was asking His disciples, 'Who do people say that the Son of Man is?' And they said, 'Some say John the Baptist; and others, Elijah; but still others, Jeremiah, or one of the prophets.' He said to them 'But who do you say that I am?' Simon Peter answered, 'You are the Christ, the Son of the living God.' And Jesus said to him, 'Blessed are you, Simon Barjona, because flesh and blood did not reveal this to you, but My Father who is in heaven. I also say to you that you are Peter, and upon this rock

> I will build My church (*ecclesia*); and the gates of Hades will not overpower it. I will give to you the keys of the kingdom of heaven; and whatever you bind on earth shall have been bound in heaven, and whateveryou loose on earth shall have been loosed in heaven.'"

Matthew 16:13-19

Ecclesia, the Greek word used by Jesus, is the term used throughout the New Testament which we translate into the English word "church". The *ecclesia* was the governing institution established by the ancient Greek city-states in the seventh century B.C. to oversee their political economies, their social institutions, and national defense. While these institutions carried within them the citizens' national philosophical and religious sentiments, they were not religious organizations. They were governing bodies much like the modern day governing institutions of democratic societies. They were remarkably unlike "church" as we know it today. Indeed, the powerful grip of religion (man's attempt to discover and please God through rules, regulations, and man's own efforts) has attempted to hide the true meaning and function of Christ's *ecclesia,* turning it into a religious institution from its inception.

So let us commence this critical discussion concerning this *ecclesia* which Christ pronounced to be the institution holding and operating the keys to the Kingdom of God. This is the most important conversation within this book and speaks to all the economic issues of this book and far more; it holds within it the ability to define and outline both the process and strategy of discipling the nations and the further clarification of the nature and functions of the church itself in that process.

As a word, *ecclesia* carried four history-changing concepts within it for both the Jews and the entirety of mankind: 1) It carried a measure of linguistic continuity within it, linking itself to the historical Jewish religion; 2) It was an almost unthinkable departure from the meaning and practices of the Jewish synagogue; 3) It was inclusive in that it forced the Jews to consider God's commitment to bringing Gentiles into His covenant they falsely believed to be exclusively their own; and 4) By its very historical nature and practice, it redefined the spiritual role of God's people to a much, much broader role in the influence of surrounding cultures and political-economic systems than they had ever considered to be their "spiritual" assignments.

Before we discuss the other major issues I have just raised, permit me to quickly cover the first point of the above paragraph regarding the linguistic issues posed by the use of the word *ecclesia* in the context of Christ's Jewish listeners. While I am no language expert relative to these ancient languages, I have availed myself of others who are. Although we only have record of Jesus using *ecclesia* three times Himself, the Holy Spirit oversaw its usage over 100 times in the New Testament. This is in contrast to the other uses that described Christ's followers, such as "body", used forty times, and "bride", used twenty times. *Ecclesia* is a word composed of the Greek words *ek* and *kaleo,* which denoted the calling together of those citizens set apart to sit in governance within the council of the *ecclesia.* These "called-out" citizens were operating within the boundaries of their city-states' constitutions, which should give us as believers a clear picture of our roles as citizens of God's Kingdom operating within the context of the Scriptures as our constitution. *Ekkleo* specifies one called to a specific duty. The Old Testament (Hebrew) words used to speak to the assembling together of the people or their leaders were *Qahal* (pronounced kaw-HAWL), and `*edah* (pronounced ay-DAW). Other words were infrequently used. The point here is that the assembling together of the leaders or people to hear or adjudicate was certainly not a new idea to the Jewish people, but to use the Gentile word *ecclesia* would have been an abrasive departure at best, and a near blasphemy at worst, because it implied that God's covenant people of Israel would assemble under a Gentile identity.

As for touching on another major issue, noted above as issue number two, the use of the word *ecclesia* by Jesus to describe His ruling institution, rather than the word "synagogue", would have been nearly incomprehensible to His followers if by that He meant the replacement of the synagogue with the Gentile "dog's" *ecclesia.* Matthew 16:13-19 gives us no indication of how the disciples heard this term *ecclesia,* although it was clearly a term they were familiar with since it was used commonly throughout the Mediterranean basin as a borrowed form of government by the Roman Empire.[5] What is absolutely clear is that the whole early *ecclesia* of Jewish believers initially fought against the idea of an inclusive embracing of the Gentile world. They embraced it with great difficulty, even after Peter's experience and testimony,[6] as well as the apostle Paul's early successes with the Gentile *ecclesiae.*

May I say this with the gravest of concerns and convictions: The demonic spirit of religion which occupied the religious Jews and their synagogues of Christ's day has had a firm grip on much of the *ecclesia* since it sprang forth after Christ's resurrection. Old demonic forces don't just fade away; they simply dress in contemporary clothing. The modern church is plagued far more than it knows with this major demonic prince, keeping us contained by religious trappings and abhorring true involvement with the influence and leavening of culture, political policies, and the economic foundations of managing the earth and its resources. Most significantly, this *ecclesia* is to be nourished by relationships with God and man rather than rules of behavior that only feed man's frustrations or give him a false sense of security when he manages to obey some of them.

Regarding the third major issue raised by the use of *ecclesia* by Jesus, the word itself denoted to His disciples an inclusive spirit rather than an exclusive spirit so tenaciously held to by the Jews of His day. Once again, I must raise the issue of the exclusive spirit of the synagogue gripping so much of the *ecclesia* throughout history. I am quite clear on the scriptural lines of being inside of Christ's covenant and outside of it. I am not talking about being saved or lost, so to speak. I am talking about an exclusive spirit that believers wear that sets them apart from all others in such a manner that it repels people and reeks of unmerited pride, as the religious leader who prayed, "God, I thank thee that I am not as other men are."[7] May God deliver His people

---

5. Acts 19:30, 33, 39. (All these words translated as "assembly" were in fact the Greek word *ecclesia,* the common form of local civic rule in Christ's time.)
6. Acts 10:45.
7. Luke 18:11, KJV.

from this spirit of exclusivity and make us as our Master who was a friend of sinners and wore no such cloak of superiority.

As we look at the fourth of the major implications of Christ's usage of *ecclesia,* we now return once again to the core reality and methodology of discipling nations and rendering unto Him that for which He died. The concept of the *ecclesia* and its historical work and records clearly tell us that its purview of activities was the caring for the whole of the culture and nation's welfare. This I personally know by virtue of my study of this institution at length during my university tenure at Berkeley in the 1960s. As a point of meaningful digression, when I as a nonbeliever at Berkeley, discovered that the word "church" came from the Greek word *ecclesia,* I could hardly believe it—the gap and the disconnect were too great. My passion since the early 1970s has been to help the *ecclesia* rediscover its identity and "walk out on the water" of discipling nations by engaging their grief, sorrows, and muddled attempts to create social systems that love God and neighbor alike. So here we are. The *ecclesia* must act out of its true identity and disciple nations through taking spiritual authority under Christ over His earth, engaging local communities with service, leadership, and compassion, and bring scriptural principles and values to the political economies of the world. So, time being limited here, let us move on to the practices of what the headlines of this discussion means.

DISCIPLING NATIONS FROM THE FOUNDATIONS UP:
THE *ECCLESIA* AND SPIRITUAL STRONGHOLDS
—CORD NUMBER ONE—

"What God has planned for the church in this hour is greater than our ability to imagine and pray. We must have the help of the Holy Spirit to learn about these mysteries of the Church and God's Kingdom. Without Him we don't have enough insight even to know what to ask for in prayer."

Bill Johnson, *When Heaven Invades Earth*, 2005, p. 177

Many people believe that transforming a nation is essentially a political thing and that we should properly focus on discipling a nation by directing our primary energy at the senior levels of public policy makers who lead our nations. While we must indeed focus on this arena as one of the three principal methodologies of transforming nations, this specific activity is actually carried out by a relatively few number of people whose ministries and engiftments qualify them to do so. I remind us once again that while the world system tells us that change comes from the top down, and the outside in (through laws and political strategies by the elite), in the Kingdom we know that change comes from the grass roots up, and the inside out (by changing the hearts of people, thereby changing their values). For us, we must begin where the invisible battle for the nations begins: on the spiritual levels of prayer and the displacement of Satan's leadership over the ideologies of the people and spiritual strongholds over the land. This takes us then to the issues concerning the church, or more properly, the true nature of the *ecclesia.*

An essential part of the lifestyle and function of the *ecclesia* deals with our ability to function in the realm of the so-called "supernatural."[8] Before we engage the discussion of the *ecclesia's* role in displacing the authority of the demonic princes overseeing us, let us briefly discuss the other critical issues of functioning in the Spirit within the *ecclesia.* They are, but are not limited to, the following major activities:

1. The *ecclesia* must preach the *kerygma* (the proclamations) of the Gospel by the power of the Holy Spirit,[9] while its people and leaders live and function in the Spirit as a lifestyle.

2. The *ecclesia* must recognize and endeavor to be constantly up-grading their worldview to a Kingdom point of view, which is spiritually evaluated rather than naturally evaluated by simple logic or reason. Revelation, or illumination, as some speak of it is

8.   Mark 16:15-18; Acts 12:7; 19:11.
9.   Romans 1:16.

spiritually assessed rather than intellectually assessed. We cannot disciple nations without this.[10]

3. The *ecclesia* must regularly come together to worship together in the Spirit, as praise and worship refresh and empower the believers.[11]

4. The *ecclesia* must seek to increasingly experience the Spirit's work and power in the realm of spiritual gifts, divine healing, and the working of miracles. These outworkings of God's Kingdom are essential to the realms of both evangelism and the elevating of the saints' faith, in living and moving in the eternal realms of God in the current dimension of time.[12]

5. The *ecclesia* must move in the realm of spiritual power in their personal and corporate prayer lives.[13]

6. The *ecclesia* must disciple its people and model community, passing on to every generation all of the above mandates.

Now we are ready to resume our discussion concerning the *ecclesia* and its role in spiritual warfare. As we noted in chapter 3, man, in Adam, lost control of the planet in the spiritual realm when he disobeyed God and Satan apparently parceled out the earth into territories, wherein his minions exercise their controlling and disrupting influences over people, systems, and the work of the *ecclesia* in particular. As we also noted there, ideologies and cultural sins are "glued in place" so to speak, within cultures and people groups. Particular types of sin also become rampant in certain cultures, families, and geographical areas. We cited 2 Corinthians 10:3-5 there as well, wherein the apostle Paul reminds us that the ideologies of man are empowered in the spiritual realm by demonic personalities, and we believers cannot be truly effective in the world until they are first subdued.

---

10. 1 Corinthians 2:1-16.
11. Hebrews 10:25; 1 Corinthians 14:26.
12. 1 Corinthians 12:1-11.
13. Jude 1:20.

While this is not the place to go into this realm in depth, let me make several key observations at this juncture. Firstly, these demonic "princes" are major forces in the hierarchy of created beings called "the majestic ones" or "angelic majesties" in the book of Jude, verse 8. Those who would encounter them must follow the protocols of God in dealing with them as the next verse in Jude admonishes us. This whole issue of dealing with principalities, powers, and rulers in high places is a calling that the *ecclesia* indeed has but one which requires great caution and deliberate energy.

What is clear to me scripturally is that those believers, specifically called to a specific local *ecclesia* in a specific geographical location,[14] are the ones most empowered to deal with them under the guidance of mature apostolic or prophetic leadership. The whole concept of the *ecclesia* is based upon those local citizens serving in it taking spiritual authority over the land where they are committed to live and rule. In other words, we have authority where we have assigned commitments. This concept has massive implications as to the actual legitimacy of who is and is not a true member of a local church. The issue is not joining the local congregation; the issue then becomes, are you and yours actually assigned by the Holy Spirit to that local *ecclesia?* Biblically speaking, I cannot see any other qualification for true authority in a local congregation other than divine placement rather than human placement. After all, ultimately it is Christ's *ecclesia* and not ours and He has declared, "He will build His church" and "God has placed the members, each one of them, in the body, just as He desired."[15] Pastors and church leaders who continue to pour life and energy into those in their churches who are there by human choice should be advised of the peril to their health and well-being. The burnout among current leaders makes my point.

What we do know for sure is that the current social-economic crisis has "shelled" the nations and softened up the ground in terms of confidence in their faith in secular reason and their ability to produce both social

---

14. 1 Corinthians 12:18.
15. Matthew 16:18; 1 Corinthians 12:18.

cohesion and sustainable prosperity. This is a clear prophetic signal for the local churches to become true *ecclesiae* and begin to displace social-spiritual values in the natural realms, by dealing with them first and vigorously in the spiritual realms. Over the next decades the realities and actual track records of our work in *ecclesia* rulership will grow rapidly around the world. The results will range from exciting to breathtaking.

DISCIPLING NATIONS WITH CRITICAL MASS
—CORD NUMBER TWO—

"The LORD loves the gates of Zion more than
all the other dwelling places of Jacob."

Psalm 87:2

In the 1980s I personally spent seven years and nearly a million air miles working to help local churches in the United States become *ecclesiae* and multi-jurisdictional servants of the Kingdom. I was trying to turn their leaders and the leaders of their cities back to the city gates, in a unified and joint commitment to enhance cities through the efforts of both the private sector and values that mobilize people to serve and care for their community. Of the thirty-plus cities that I and my colleagues served, many took our seed-planting and proceeded to make exciting progress that continues today.

Israel is not only a model to study relative to social and economic structures, it serves as a biblical picture of political structures and the role of civil government as well. Those who say that their religion is a "private thing" are often right; their faith is indeed religious and their lack of study of the Scriptures relative to social systems keeps them ignorant of the rich social dimensions of truth found there. As any serious student of Western political science knows, Western social structures and legal systems were patterned off the Scriptures principally as much as if not more than Greek or Roman experiences. Having studied these things with other biblical educators, lawyers, and social scientists, all of our historic social structures in the United States were overwhelming initially patterned off scriptural systems set in the Old and New Testaments. It is both amusing and exasperating to hear secular leaders attempt to revise history and tell a different story.

Unfortunately, in the dumbing down of American education we now have large numbers of teachers abysmally ignorant of these realities, and hence their students are equally clueless.

The pattern of ancient Israel, in terms of its governing civil structures, was startlingly decentralized relative to the civil structures of the modern state. As we have already noted in this book, the patterns of secular society are increasingly centralized as civil government continues to extend its grasp over larger and larger dimensions of its citizens' lives and choices. This is not a "conservative" political opinion but rather an absolute sociological fact. However, as also noted repeatedly in this book, we have discussed the economic fact that as civil government is defunded by its bankrupting, overextension of its governmental reach, the crisis is pressing the cultures back toward more local authority and required responsibility from the private sector. This is the open door of course for the *ecclesia* to once again serve their cultures as the early church served its Roman culture by saving the lives of children and the aged, and starting educational programs, Christian-based legal services, food services, and a host of other acts of Kingdom charity which ultimately gave them the hearts of the people.

A term called "mediating structures" emerged some years back in a book by Peter L. Berger and Richard John Neuhaus, which talks about society being held together by social ties between the individual and the State through voluntary associations within the private sector.[16] This web of mediating entities involves a significant set of social structures that helps us understand society as an association of associations. This picture is helpful and speaks to how the French social scientist Alexis de Tocqueville viewed the core strength of American society in the 1800s, as being uniquely powerful due to the web of private sector organizations interfacing with the individuals and the civil government. The democratic society, in this dimension, can therefore be measured as to its social health by the number and effectiveness of social organizations operating to meet the needs of the citizens beyond the institution of centralized civil government. This decentralized web of

---

16. Peter L. Berger and Richard John Neuhaus, *To Empower People: The Role of Mediating Structures in Public Policy* (Washington, DC: AEI Press, 1977).

active associations is a hedge against the ruling elites of both the private sector and civil government. It speaks to the dictum, "whoever serves most effectively, leads" which is a reality every social strategist knows to be true.[17] This is why historically all authoritarian states and centralized government strategists immediately attempt to shut down service of any educational institutions within society other than themselves.

CITY ACTION COUNCILS FACILITATE
COMMUNITY-DRIVEN CHRISTIAN INVOLVEMENT

The "City Action Councils" I was facilitating in the 1980s were defined as voluntary associations of local community leaders who meet regularly to strategize, pray, and mobilize those they lead and influence to engage in meeting the needs of their communities. Each council was locally controlled and funded, and comprised the joint cooperation of church leaders, the business community, service organizations, ministries, and leaders from the civil government who clearly saw the advantages of social services and funding that helped to meet the needs of their community. We put together a manual on how to begin these councils, operate them, and encouraged them to explore for themselves how to most effectively operate as they went along.

Our strategic input involved helping their leaders to:

1. Analyze and assess community needs and resources.

2. Build intercessory prayer networks.

3. Provide mediation services for community needs and problems.

4. Promote effective dialogues and communication with local officials and community organizations.

5. Raise needed resources for programs and aid that meet the needs of the homeless, aged, and youth of the community.

6. Serve as organizers for disaster preparation for the community.

---

17. Luke 22:24-27.

7. Organize mass cleanup campaigns for communities, where citizens can accomplish hundreds of thousands of dollars of cleanups in a single day.

8. Encourage the adopting of neighborhoods and provide services for those having needs within them.

9. Hold "Honoring Excellence Celebrations" for local politicians, police, and social services people who did exemplary things within the community or state in an attempt to make effective service in the community a highly esteemed and celebrated community value.

The list could go on and on but our core idea was to utilize God's "Master Plan of Global Renewal" given to us all in Genesis 2:15, which is to care for and tend the relational "garden" He has set us in. Everyone has a "garden" comprised of our natural families, our spiritual families, those we work with, our friends, and those in the community with whom we engage on either a regular or even "divine encounter" basis. The world surely would be renewed and served if every believer simply prayed into and served those in their gardens with the vigor and real demonstrations of Christ's love and provision.

The discipling of nations, to use a military term, requires "boots on the ground." Powerful prayer by those anointed to do battle with the spiritual princes is essential but not that many are called to do so. Sustained and effective prayer for community needs by the masses of believers will turn the local churches into biblical *ecclesiae* that overcome the gates of hell that torment and dehumanize the citizens of the community. Those called to serve as elected civil officials or give wise counsel to the establishment of just laws and sustainable prosperity for the greatest number of people is wonderful, but only a relative few are called and equipped to do so. Yet, the millions of believers of the nations' *ecclesiae* are boots on the ground for service. They are the display of viable communities actually working within the Christian community and evangelism and the realm of the power of God. These believers validate not only His existence but the values He sets forth that lead to personal and social freedom. To disciple nations, we ideally need every believer to see and recognize their place on the wall and their seat on a local *ecclesia* wherein God has placed them.[18] Though we may never get this fullness of spiritual participation, we will indeed get enough to do the job because God has decreed it and His bride will indeed make herself ready.[19] Through our boots on the ground these Scriptures will be fulfilled:

"Then they will rebuild the ancient ruins, They will raise up the former devastations; And they will repair the ruined cities, The desolations of many generations."

Isaiah 61:4

"They will not hurt or destroy in all My holy mountain, For the earth will be full of the knowledge of the LORD As the waters cover the sea. Then in that day The nations will resort to the root of Jesse, who will stand as a signal for the peoples; And His resting place will be glorious."

Isaiah 11:9-10

DISCIPLING THE NATIONS: INFLUENCING POLICY AND AFFECTING VALUES, HEARTS, AND MINDS —CORD NUMBER THREE—

As already noted, those called to run for public office and serve in these capacities on multiple levels are a relatively few number of believers. While many can serve on councils, committees, and social services leadership positions, not a large multitude will serve in the more complicated offices requiring special skill sets or educational training and experience. Multitudes can and should be managers and leaders where they work, and large numbers can own and operate their own businesses and greatly influence their community for the Kingdom. The most significant point here once again is that in the Kingdom there are no little people or people whose contributions are of no value. Nevertheless, some will be captains of industry or multi-millionaires

---

18. Nehemiah 4:1-13.
19. Revelation 19:7.

or billionaires who shape major social institutions or philanthropic organizations of large size.

While we could go into language strategy and a host of other essential skills to be used in the process of social change and political and economic organizing and influence, time does not allow that discussion to proceed here. What most needs to be said here is that those who are called to be socially and politically influential need to strategically come together and set about availing ourselves of this unique historical opportunity, given to us by the economic crisis and its attendant "gifts" to those who know what to do with them. Certainly my attempt to discuss some of the fundamental and basic issues of Kingdom economic perspectives here in this book is my small public contribution to this process. What have always hindered us greatly in the body of Christ are our divisions, competitiveness, and general lack of strategically directed actions. It often appears that we are, as a people, as inept as some of our critics paint us to be. There is great pain in these words since we allegedly represent Christ in these matters as in all others. Suffice to say, if we fail to avail ourselves of this current opportunity we will need to profusely apologize to our Master, our progeny, and the people of the earth bereft of an opportunity for true change by our ineptitude. Those who hear this sound will indeed show up and they will make a difference.

It will take a significant mobilization of at least 10 percent of the churches' envisioned and committed believers deploying this kind of threefold strategic engagement to truly alter a nation. Inherent in this mobilization is Paul's statement regarding the abiding power of faith, hope, and love permeating this spiritual activism.[20] So, we are back to the beginning: Love God fervently, and love your neighbor redemptively. The Greatest Commandment stands unaltered, relevant, and effectual.[21]

---

20. 1 Corinthians 13:13.
21. Matthew 22:36-40.

IN CONCLUSION

"All the ends of the earth will remember and turn to the LORD,
And all the families of the nations will worship before You. For
the kingdom is the LORD's, And He rules over the nations."

Psalm 22:27-28

God has not brought history to this point without a purpose. His inevitable glory and the glory of His Son and His Kingdom will be furthered by this current situation. The machinations of man also serve the purposes of God, since He bends all things to His will and uses the energies of His enemies to further His own purposes. The will and necessity of addressing our social systems in general, and economic realities in particular, must be done in every discipline of man and his culture. We are in this values and economic crisis every bit as much because we Christians have failed to perform our role in God's world, as the world systems' ineptitude has placed us here. May God forgive us. And may a people-loving *ecclesia* globally arise and bring Christ the glory for which He paid. Let His bride take her rightful place as a servant of our Father and a lover of mankind. The question now remains: What will you and I do to effectively play our part in seizing this wonderful and immensely challenging opportunity?

> "But if we and our posterity reject religious instruction and authority, violate the rules of eternal justice, trifle with the injunctions of morality, and recklessly destroy the political constitution which holds us together, no man can tell how sudden a catastrophe may overwhelm us, that shall bury all our glory in profound obscurity. Should that catastrophe happen, let it have no history! Let that horrible narrative never be written!"

Daniel Webster,
*Address Delivered Before the New York
Historical Society,* February 23, 1852

ABOUT THE AUTHOR

Dennis Peacocke's life and concerns for social justice and political-economic freedom were largely defined while attending and graduating from the University of California at Berkeley in the field of political theory amidst the turmoil of the 1960s. From there, he worked as a research assistant to labor unions and was a business owner. He unexpectedly encountered Christ in 1968. Since then he has pastored, worked with church networks and traveled extensively around the world lecturing on applied theology, business, economics, and the relationship between current events and the Kingdom of God. The author of four books, he is sought out as a passionate voice for the spiritual foundations undergirding freedom, prosperity, and community.

He and his wife, Jan, live in Santa Rosa, California. They have three married children and eleven grandchildren.

STRATEGIC CHRISTIAN SERVICES

Where and how will you make a difference in this crisis/opportunity?

For more information on how you can practically contribute and be a part of the solution go to www.gostrategic.org or call our offices at **707-578-7700 or 800-700-0605.**

- Get further informed

- Get further trained

- Get connected and positioned